I
Only
Have
a Minute

ALSO BY KATHY BROWN

Living Happily Ever Laughter
A Guide to Thinking Funny in a Face-Paced World

I Only Have a Minute ...

So Let's Make It Matter!

By
Kathy Brown

Energetic ExPress
Woodbury, Minnesota 55125 U.S.A.

ISBN-13: 978-0-9743886-1-8
ISBN-10: 0-9743886-1-0

Published in the United States of America by
    Energetic ExPress
    888.524.5194
    651.730.1109
    www.kathybrown.com

Cover Design by George Foster of Foster Covers

Editing and Production Coordination by Carol Pettitt Communications, Inc.

Contents

Acknowledgments

I would like to first thank my beloved daughter, Julie, and her incredible husband, John, who have endured so much but rose to each challenge with love, hope, prayer, and each other. Thank you for letting me share your journey in hopes that others will draw strength from it and trust the Lord completely no matter what the outcome. Thanks to Dr. Karen Drake and Dr. Paula Mahone, who were my daughter's physicians. They cared for her as if she were their very own daughter through her multiple pregnancies. Dr. Mahone uttered the words that became encrypted on my brain: "You Only Have A Minute." The idea and name of this book were conceived at that profound moment when our world suddenly stood still.

Thank you, Carol Pettitt, for your constant encouragement and affirmation as I wrote and you edited. Your friendship and talent were truly a gift from God! A special thanks to George Foster who designed the cover, which continually inspired me as I wrote. Your patience and professionalism meant so much! A heartfelt thanks to Jan Boettcher, my dear friend from high school, who has always believed in me and thought the best. She is a living example of God's loving patience because we both know that He isn't finished with us yet! The BEST is yet to come! Maybe we will get even cuter?

It has been said that we become who we are because of those who love us. I want to thank my husband and soul mate, Ken, who has allowed me to become who I am today. Thanks for your constant applause of unconditional love!

My greatest thanks goes to the author of life, my LORD. He gets a standing ovation! He made me, loves me, and has given me the opportunity to share this book with all of you. May God use your life mightily in ways that really matter ... even if you only have a minute!

Dedication

This book was born, after a great deal of pain, to leave a legacy of love and laughter in honor of my grandchildren, Katie Lynn, Matthew John, and Natalie Lynn. They generated an incredible outpouring of love, in a very brief period of time, from those who knew them and prayed for them. We held them for moments in our hands and, now, forever in our hearts. Their brief lives made an incredible impact!

Before this book was completed, another angel baby, Jacob Wesley, attempted to make a live entrance into this world with his twin brother, Samuel John, by his side. After six months of life inside my daughter's womb, Jacob's spirit returned to heaven to be with his other brother and sisters.

This book is now dedicated not only to the triplets but also to the memory of Jacob Wesley. They are all now playing together in heaven. I know there is a playground there where children run, play, laugh, and sing together while praising our Father who lives there with them and who loves them with a love that goes beyond our human understanding.

This book was a labor of love. I hope you enjoy the delivery!

Chapter One
The Power of a Moment

This book is about the art of living fully in every moment you are alive. It is about experiencing more meaning in the short sound bites of time you spend with others. You will discover there is energy in enthusiasm when you allow yourself to be more available to meet the needs of others and experience the joy that this brings.

According to the World Book Dictionary, a "moment" is "a very short space of time; an instant." How significant can something that short be? I am often amazed at the joy obtained in brief encounters with others. We miss so much of the joy because we choose not to be engaged with others, even for a moment. What a loss for all concerned!

Being open to connect with people whether it is at a garage sale or a grocery store could mean the difference between receiving a huge blessing or experiencing just another day.

"Connecting" with people is very important whether you know them or not. Abe Lincoln said, "Strangers are only friends that you haven't met yet." The world is full of new friends for us if only we will take one tiny moment to connect with them in some way. I tend to meet people who make a significant impact on my life in the strangest places! Recently, I was due for my mammogram so I took my breasts to, you guessed it, the Hospital

I Only Have a Minute ... So Let's Make It Matter!

Breast Center. I happened to be the only one waiting to have a mammogram at that time when suddenly the door from inside the clinic opened and an elderly Hmong woman walked into the waiting room where I was sitting. As I watched her emerge, I wondered whether she spoke English. I flashed a warm smile to acknowledge her presence.

She looked over, saw my glance, and walked directly over to me. "Hi, I am 83," she said, looking me straight in the eye to see what my reaction would be. I continued to smile and countered with the fact that getting to be 83 was quite an accomplishment. She then pointed to both of her breasts, one at a time, while she continued, seriously. "They're good," she said, looking quite pleased. I smiled inside, thinking, "good breast, good breast" ... that's pretty cute. What would you do to punish a bad breast? Oh well, I digress. The medical mind has strange ways of thinking funny to keep the little sanity we can claim some days.

I recognized her diagnosis and responded, "That's great! Your tests are negative and everything is fine?"

I smiled broadly as I pondered how one would take care of breasts. Maybe making sure they are clean, dry, and get out now and then? How do you really "take care" of them? Could they sue you for neglect? I only ask because I try to keep abreast of things.

I looked this precious lady straight in the eyes and said with a full heart, "I celebrate with you that your breasts are good and that your tests turned out well." She smiled broadly, pulled the ties on her scarf a little tighter and replied, "Thank you! Bye, bye." She turned and went out of my life, but will forever remain in my heart. Tears came to my eyes because she had chosen to share her good news with me and my breasts. We were both blessed.

What if I had looked down or started to thumb through a magazine so I looked busy and unapproachable? I would have missed a wonderful moment that I will long remember.

The Power of a Moment

Can you think of some moments in your life that made a difference in someone else's life because you were aware? Think back to people you have met where your connection with them became significant right away or at a later date. I never would have thought that someone I met while having a garage sale could have such a large impact on so many people. Let me tell you the "Tale of the Sale."

I promised my family I would have another garage sale so we could trade our past treasures and trash for cash. Included in the sale were some "interesting" flowered draperies that my younger son had taken off the windows of his newly purchased town home. During the heat of the sale I heard a woman exclaim, "Oh, what lovely draperies!" I immediately was drawn to the lady who made this statement. She then continued, "We are missionaries just back from Thailand, and we don't have any drapes on our windows. The padding on the back would sure keep out the cold."

The medical mind has strange ways of thinking funny to keep the little sanity we can claim some days.

Her sweet spirit was so apparent as she looked practically at the drapes. I told her that she could have them for half price. She was totally thrilled, gathered them up with a sweet smile of gratitude, and happily left with her husband.

The next day as my husband and I were putting leftover items into boxes to donate, I saw the missionary husband coming up the driveway with a young teenager. The teen was a handsome young man who greeted us with a smile and warm hello which revealed an obvious cleft palate.

The older man explained that he had seen a golf bag here the day before that he thought his adopted son, Rosen, from Bulgaria would love. Rosen said he worked as a golf caddy at a local golf course that I was familiar with. His eyes lit up as he explored the bag closely. "How much is it?" he asked. "Three dollars," his dad replied. The young man then asked his father if he could have his allowance early, to which his dad agreed, pulling out three one-dollar bills. Rosen started to hand me the three dollars when I clasped his hand and said, "Just keep it and get yourself something else."

His expression turned to joy as he started down our driveway, almost dancing, with a huge smile on his face. He repeated, "Thank you lady, thank you so much!" I then called out to him that he could have anything else he saw before we packed up. The father also called out to his son and repeated my offer, but he didn't hear either one of us. His dad sighed and smiled broadly, explaining that his son was so thrilled with the new golf bag that he couldn't think about anything else!

It really struck me how genuinely grateful this young man was for something as simple as a used golf bag. He was content with what he had received, and desired nothing else. This teenager was living a great biblical principal before our very eyes.

Philippians 4:12: "I know what it is to be in need, and I know what it is to have plenty. I have learned the secret of being content in any and every situation."

That night as I lay in bed I kept thinking about how grateful that young man was. God seemed to whisper in my ear how much he loved the people who serve Him so unselfishly and expect little, if anything, in return like this missionary family I had the honor of meeting at this "whale of a sale." I thought how great it would be if, one day, Rosen had his mouth fixed so he could tell others, with even more confidence, about God's amazing love and provision.

The Power of a Moment

My thoughts continued as I visited my dentist, Dr. Kyle Edlund, the next week. I told him the garage sale story and asked him if he had ever partnered in helping out someone with limited resources. He looked at me intently, paused for just a moment, and then said with a warm smile, "If you can find him, I will treat him." My heart leapt with joy thinking of how this young teenager's self esteem and future could be impacted by a true professional whose heart was open and obedient to hearing and acting upon God's call.

I contacted the caddy master at the golf course asking if he had a caddy there with a cleft palate. The man acted very protective asking why I wanted to know. I told him the garage sale story and how a few of us felt led to help this young man get his teeth fixed. The manager softened immediately as he affirmed what a beautiful thing that would be.

> He was content with what he had received, and desired nothing else.

He shared that Rosen had received "Caddy of the Year" this past year because of his excellent attitude going that extra mile in service to others at the golf course. Everyone adored him.

When I called Rosen's number, his adopted mother answered. I told her I was the "garage sale drape lady," and I was calling to tell her that God had laid it on my heart to find help for Rosen's mouth. She had tears in her voice as she shared that the timing was certainly the Lord's. Two days earlier Rosen had had three teeth pulled at a hospital where students get experience by performing procedures for people with lower incomes at no charge.

The hospital had called about three hours after the surgery saying they had pulled a wrong tooth and wanted Rosen to come back so they could try to put it back in. The tooth was reinserted, but Rosen was so discouraged and in so much pain that he decided to trust God with his mouth instead of dentists! God heard his cry and changed his heart, so Rosen finally agreed to be seen by Dr. Edlund following his awesome offer.

My generous dentist not only examined, cleaned, and x-rayed Rosen's teeth, but he also consulted with an orthodontist and an oral surgeon. Before Christmas that year, Rosen received a full set of braces along with ongoing care from true professionals who wanted to make a difference in this young man's life.

> I truly believe that 'coincidences' are God's way of remaining anonymous.

Everyone I met who was a part of the team helping Rosen had a glow about the whole experience. They took extra pains to ensure that Rosen and his family understood all that was being done by demonstrating how to maintain the work for the most positive outcome. Through the loving thoroughness of caring professionals, Rosen overcame his past fears of having his mouth worked on. He made many friends who found joy in making a difference in this young man's life.

I truly believe that "coincidences" are God's way of remaining anonymous. Rosen is now with YWAM (Youth With A Mission) in a ministry to help street children. He told me he was an orphan until the age of 12 when he was adopted and brought to America. He said he ate rice a couple of times a day and that, as a growing boy, he would occasionally eat a bird to survive. Now that is literally "fast food." You had to be fast and hungry to do that! God had prepared a grateful heart in Rosen, who radiated sincere appreciation for whatever God provided in his life. What a testimony of God's amazing love and concern for His children's needs. His eye is on the sparrow even when it becomes someone's lunch.

The Power of a Moment

Keep on loving each other as brothers. Do not forget to entertain strangers, for by so doing some people have entertained angels without knowing it. (Hebrews 13:1-2)

I feel like I entertained an angel at my garage sale that summer. The moment I decided to give away – not sell – that golf bag, life changed, not only for Rosen, but for all those who then had the opportunity to give of themselves with their own unique gifts to an act of kindness bigger than themselves.

If you still are not convinced that moments can count immeasurably, ask an Olympian who finished one tenth of a second behind another contestant. That miniscule amount of time resulted in the difference between being remembered for an incredible achievement or having accomplished something equally as incredible but being rewarded less – all because of a tenth of a second!

Short amounts of time where you are delayed by simple mishaps can either take your life or save it as the following accounts demonstrate:

> **Do not forget to entertain strangers, for by so doing, some people have entertained angels without knowing it.**
> *- Heb. 13:2*

The head of a company survived 9/11 because his son started kindergarten that day. Another fellow was alive because it was his turn to bring donuts. One woman was late because her alarm clock didn't go off in time. One missed his bus. One spilled food on her clothes and had to take time to change. One went back to answer the telephone. One had a child who dawdled and didn't get ready in time. One story that struck me involved the man wearing a new pair of shoes to work, but before he got there he developed a blister on his foot and had to stop at a drugstore to buy a Band-Aid.

Next time little things happen like being stuck in traffic, missing the elevator, or driving behind a slow person in the fast lane, I will think to myself, "This is exactly where God wants me to be at this very moment." He has a divine plan, and we have choices as to how we react to the positive and negative moments that come into our lives.

The reason for this book is because of a series of "Moments That Mattered" in my life that have changed me and my family forever. Let me give you a peek inside my heart as I share what happened.

> Next time little things happen, like being stuck in traffic, I will think to myself,
> 'This is exactly where God wants me to be at this very moment.'

My only daughter, Julie, and her husband, John, were so looking forward to having a family. Due to some physical problems, they needed some assistance to accomplish their dream. They persevered with a strong faith, trusting in God's perfect timing. When they told us they were not only pregnant, but they were having triplets, the thought of an instant family with three children was pretty overwhelming. Every cell in my body began celebrating.

Being the quiet, shy grandmother that I am NOT, anyone who stood near me even for a moment had a very good chance of finding out that my daughter was pregnant with triplets. The way I see it, joy should be shared and share we all did! Whenever meeting friends, there were the usual greetings, and then the next question would be about the progress of the triplets. After two showers for these little people, anticipation was rising.

The Power of a Moment

At 21 weeks gestation, Julie called me during tornado warnings to share news that was more ominous than the weather. Contractions had started and she was in the hospital frantically trying to understand what was happening and why. She was undoubtedly questioning herself, "What did I do, what should I have done, and what could I have done to prevent this unexpected turn of events?" She said Dr. Mahone had told her the first baby was coming and would arrive in about an hour and a half and there wasn't anything they could do to stop it at this point. The baby, they said, did not have a chance to survive.

My husband and I immediately jumped into the car to make the seemingly endless four-hour drive. We kept taking refuge under viaducts as the rain pounded mercilessly and lightening streaked across the sky. My eyes were raining and my heart was pounding with determination to get to my daughter's side. I thought of a mama bear and how fiercely she protects her young. I wanted to protect Julie from the emotional and physical pain she was experiencing, but I didn't know how. Pray was all we could do as we drove with pent-up passion knowing heartbreak lay waiting for us. We called half way there only to find out that Katie Lynn, my namesake, had been born and died peacefully in her daddy's arms.

The next day we talked with my daughter's physicians, Dr. Karen Drake and Dr. Paula Mahone, who had delivered the McCaughey septuplets in Iowa in 1997. I asked how many multiple-birth babies they had delivered where the first one died and the other two lived. They said none. But there was a 10 percent to 15 percent chance Julie's two babies could live, according to national statistics. I said that we would help these physicians become even more famous, because Julie's and John's babies were going to live! The doctors said they were totally committed to making that happen, and that two weeks was the usual turning point which would determine whether the other babies would make it or not.

It wasn't meant to be. Natalie Lynn and Matthew John joined their sister two weeks later in heaven, as our hearts broke here on earth.

> 'I believe
> I blessed them
> with my presence,
> even if my stay
> was short.'

When grief comes to visit, we all react differently. We have different outlets for the tremendous grief that is too difficult to express in mere words.

I often think of our precious grandbabies who are waiting in heaven. I have little conversations with them from my heart and imagine what they might say back in response.

"Oh, my darlings, how my heart longs to embrace you. You are elusive, kind, and loving as you brush by me and oftentimes come along side me. Ah, the brush of angel wings! Do you feel and hear them, too? Wait, I hear one of the baby angels speaking."

* * *

"Oh Nanna, I will see you again in a place where our eyes will never grow dim. Then we will be together forever and we never have to leave one another and be sad. You never got to hold me while I was alive. They named me Katie Lynn, after you, Nanna. They thought that would make you feel special because you are very special to my mom and dad. My dad hides that part pretty good because he likes to tease you, and you fall for it almost every time. He is a silly daddy.

"The nurses dressed me up so pretty in a white dress with a little pink bow between the collars when they brought out the shell of me that was left to show you when you arrived. I was already back in the arms of my heavenly Father who assured me that my work on earth had been completed.

"My heavenly Father gave me only 21 weeks of life inside my mommy, and a few moments in my mommy and daddy's arms. I know that my life mattered to them.

"I just couldn't wait, Nanna. My heavenly Father spoke softly saying He wanted me to hurry back to heaven so my mommy and daddy wouldn't feel so bad when I left. They did though. They both cried really hard. I left for heaven while lying in my earth daddy's arms, which were so strong. I felt his breath and tears on my face as he held me close. They were praying so hard that I would stay and be their little girl. My daddy is very handsome and my mommy is very beautiful! I was not fully formed so it was hard for them to really see how much I look like both of them. They made me feel beautiful while they held me close, whispering sweet sounding words. They knew I couldn't stay, but they made me feel so welcome in those moments that they held me.

So many prayers were coming to heaven, and God listened to every one of them.

"I believe I blessed them with my presence, even if my stay was short. They loved me 'really hard' for the few moments I did stay, calling me by name and holding me close. I will always love them, too! I often pray, 'Please God, let them know that my life was not in vain.' I am a part of them forever in my soul which is the part that gets to go live in heaven. It's the very best part of all of us according to my heavenly Father who knows everything.

"I left my brother, Matthew John, and my sister, Natalie Lynn, to stay inside our mother so she would still have some company. They knew they would be joining me shortly, but sent me on ahead to lead the way to heaven because I am the oldest. They wanted me to meet them at the gate of heaven so we could all be together again as soon as possible. Natalie and Matthew waited a couple of weeks so Mom and Dad could recover a little before they had to grieve again.

"We became very close in many ways as we grew in mommy's tummy. The light of God's love was with us all the time. God watched over all of us as we met briefly. So many prayers were coming to heaven, and God listened to every one of them. Hope is a gift that helps you cope in crisis, Nanna. God heard all of the prayers, but said "no" to them, as His plan is greater and will better serve the purpose He had for our lives. He really knows what's best even though no one understands it right now. 'Thy will be done on earth as it is in heaven'."

> Holding one's future in one's arms, only to have it snatched away in the moment of death, is a feeling difficult to describe, much less comprehend.

"It sure wasn't my mom's and dad's or grandparents' will that we would leave so soon. They REALLY wanted us to stay and grow up with them. I think grandparents need us really bad so they have something to laugh about and love while their bodies get old. Grandma Kathy's mind takes short vacations up here when she tries to imagine what it would be like to hug, kiss and play with us. She tries to sing to us, too, but her earthly singing voice is hopeless!

* * *

Just before Julie gave birth to Natalie and Matthew, Dr. Mahone came out and asked the grandmothers if we had any questions. My heart leaped within me, and out came the words, "May I pray for your hands?" Dr. Mahone readily agreed. Being a woman of strong faith, she said she had a lot of questions for God when she gets to heaven. She comforted us as she honestly admitted that she didn't understand why some things are allowed to happen. I prayed that God would guide her hands and that they would be gentle, swift, and efficient as they delivered our precious grandbabies whom I loved already more than words could ever say.

Who can explain the love we have for our children and grandchildren? It is from way down within our very souls. We carry the love around within us until we can set it free into acts of love. It is already there, waiting to be given to those willing to receive it, even if we only have a minute. That minute is ours to have and to hold as a sweet memory of the moments we shared. What might have been sneaks into our thinking, ripping at our hearts as we conjure up visions of the joys we might have shared if we just had more time. I set those thoughts free so as not to steal the joy of those fleeting moments that we did share.

As John and Julie looked closely at the children, John commented, "Look at Matthew's shoulders, he would have played basketball." "Look at Natalie's fingers," Julie commented lovingly. "She would have played the piano."

> Those left on earth need to live a life of love as a tribute to those gone before them.

Holding one's future in one's arms, only to have it snatched away in the moment of death, is a feeling difficult to describe, much less comprehend. There's a brief moment on the mountain top – feeling, sensing, wanting to believe it will continue. Maybe the doctors made a mistake and the babies will keep breathing.

"Come on babies, stay warm…if we only cuddle closer…Please God, please let them stay alive! Father, we are all asking, pleading, petitioning You for more time with our soon-to-be angels. Can't they stay and be loved just a little bit longer?"

God whispered, "They will always be loved. That will never end. I knew them before you did and I care about them even more than you do. I know this is hard for you to understand, but it is true. My love passes all understanding. Remember that you are only saying goodbye to their outer shell. The part that counts within them, their souls, will live forever in my kingdom. You will be with them again…they will be waiting for you. They will know you and you will know them. What a reunion that will be! You will see. The love of a mother and father for their children does not end when their life does. True love transcends life. Those left on earth need to live a life of love as a tribute to those gone before them. They need to carry the light of love in their words and actions for others to see."

> **Bad things happen to good people, but great people use those moments for a greater good.**

"Life is not fair" has been said since the beginning of time. Bad things happen to good people, but great people use those moments to accomplish an even greater good.

Katie, Matthew and Natalie only had a moment with us. They made the absolute most of it in their own way. Their parents and grandparents also only had a moment with them, and our lives will be forever impacted by those three little angels who came to visit and left their love behind for us to share with all of you.

"A child holds your hand for a while and your heart forever."

Chapter Two

Making Dollars or Sense

In America we are bombarded daily with advertising to buy something better or to get something new. "You deserve it," we are told and we tell ourselves. You should have everything you want...even if it takes a little extra time to pay for it. It is the American dream. Have it now, pay for it later, one way or another. How easy it is to get caught up in the hype that having more and better STUFF makes you feel like you are more influential and a better person as well as the envy of others. Are feelings worth going into debt for? Is it worth the pain of seemingly unending payments?

Are you driven by other people's expectations? I think Americans spend money they don't have on things they don't need to impress people they don't know. Does what other people think make or break your day? How are you affected physically, mentally and spiritually by the work you do and the money you make?

Physically: Are the physical demands required by your work in keeping with what you can deliver at this time of your life? If you are in the trades, is your 50-year-old body trying to do the work of a 25-year-old who works out at the gym?

I Only Have a Minute ... So Let's Make It Matter!

Mentally: Are the mental challenges of your work stimulating you or are they overwhelming you in a sea of stress, anxiety and discouragement?

Spiritually: Does your present job support your value system, or does it expose you to multiple gray areas of concern along with constant moral choices? When we work outside our value systems we are playing with fire...and guess who likes it hot? Answer: The guy in the red outfit with the prickly rake in his hand.

> I have never heard a resumé read at a funeral ...

You have probably heard the phrase, "Less is more," which is an interesting paradox. How can that phrase be true? It just doesn't make "sense." The premise is that contentment with less gives you more peace of mind. That does make sense. But does life always make sense? I don't think so! If you think life makes sense, is fair, and is perfectly logical, call 911 now and get yourself some help. Research will continue in the next life where the answers to all of our questions lie.

We are missing out on a significant principle that can greatly enrich our lives when we begin to understand the need to do more with less and give more than we get. This does not have to be about money, and it usually isn't. It is primarily about our time. It has been said that time is money. To some degree that is true because many of us get paid per hour. It makes sense, then, that what we invest our time in should be in direct proportion to what we value.

So what is most important in your life right now? Is it where you live, what you drive, and where you work? Or is it your faith, family, and friends? People whose lives are driven by the need to accumulate money at the expense of time with their family pay a dear price! I have never heard a resumé read at a funeral, but I have seen video clips and lots of pictures of the family having fun together.

Making Dollars or Sense

Is less really more, especially when it comes to money? Is making more money the most important aspect in measuring our success, or does making sense matter more to you because you can be content with the life you have with what you have at this moment?

We do need to make money to meet our needs, but most of us have to admit there is quite a chasm between our wants and our needs. That chasm, I have found, narrows as we mature, which some of us do quicker than others. At some point we realize that real happiness isn't in what we own but in who we are as contributing people helping others get what they need. Life is to cope with *and* contribute to. These are two important actions if you want to thrive and not just survive.

> Your true worth is in WHO you are and not in what you do, where you live, or how much you earn.

We need to ask ourselves if we are actually living our values or just talking about them. What really drives us? Are you continually looking for opportunities to make more money? When the newspaper comes to your door, do you go right to the Job Opportunities or perhaps to Market Place to look for things to buy and sell to make more money? Is EBay your "other" job?

Are you looking for a job that will offer you more money, believing this will improve your life? Have you looked closely at what those types of jobs require for that additional money? How about "No Life?" Does traveling, long hours, little sleep, and being accessible 24 hours, seven days a week sound fun and fulfilling or overwhelming? Your life should hopefully mean more to you than how much you can acquire in your "oh so short" time here on earth. Your true worth is in WHO you are and not in what you DO, where you live, or how much you earn. Oh, and while I'm asking things you love to answer…How much do you make and how much do you weigh? I think I have it covered for being annoying. Let's move on.

A speaker once shared at a professional speakers meeting a clever comeback he uses when airplane seat mates ask the proverbial, "What do you do?" and he is not in the mood to talk. He says, "I am a fund raiser for multiple charities." This tends to end the conversation quickly, and the person who asked the original question suddenly gets a huge interest in how his or her shoes look.

Another interesting response I heard when a man asked another man, "What do you do?" was, "Why do you want to know?" That seemed to me to imply, "Why is that important to you?" This may seem, to some of us, a form of confrontation. Healthy conflict is necessary for real growth and development. It may sting for a moment, but the lesson learned can make a profound difference. Listen to all corrections with an open mind even if you get a draft. That draft may blow out an out-dated paradigm that you've been hanging onto.

Dr. Robert Good was a cancer researcher known for his willingness to recognize any error in his theories and abandon them faster than anyone else in medical research. An associate said, "Dr. Good never gets married to his hypotheses, so he doesn't go through the pangs of divorce when one is proven wrong." Proverbs 9 puts a high premium on a willingness to see one's error and admit it. It describes a wise man as one who wants to learn from his mistakes. Correction becomes a faithful friend.

When I first meet someone I now ask, "What are you all about?" instead of, "What do you do?" Oftentimes people will then ask me, "What do you want to know?" I respond with, "Tell me anything you want about who you are and what matters to you." Conversations become very interesting when you let people define themselves. Some start telling me about their jobs, others start with their marital status and number of children. I have had a few talk about their love of fishing, golfing, etc. These are usually men people. Women, for the most part talk about their families, unless they are single. Then careers, education, and travel make their way into the conversation.

Relationships, I've learned, help define us. For example, I am someone's wife. Now, if you want to see one deliriously happy man…you need to meet my husband, Ken. He will say that I am just delirious…and smile. That's just one way we are different.

Men and women are not alike in a number of ways, but they are different in one rather obvious way which I think you might be interested in knowing. When men go to bed at night they wake up looking pretty much the same except for some extra whiskers.

> Conversations become very interesting when you let people define themselves.

When women go to bed, we somehow deteriorate during the night. We need all kinds of help in the morning from a vast array of products. The more mature I get the longer it is taking me to use the ever increasing number of products. The spackle sticks in the ruts of my face and it takes time to dry. While it is drying, I then have time to tweeze out those pesky hairs poking through the spackle. I am in a bit of denial about this situation and heartily agree with the woman who said, "I refuse to think of them as chin hairs. I prefer to call them runaway eyebrows." Truly, they are misguided sojourners in a tough terrain resembling weeds among the wrinkles. Did you know that one way to get rid of wrinkles is to eat until they fill in? This won't take much time especially around the Holidays, when filling up and filling out is all the rage.

We do need to "kid around" more because life's issues seem to be getting way too serious! Speaking of "kidding" around, I just came back from being with two of our boy grand-children, ages two and four, to help out for a week. While there, I found myself saying things like, "Joshua, do not put watermelon between your toes and keep your foot off the table. OK, who put the truck in the toilet?" Children keep you young and laughing as you observe their unpredictable, spontaneous behavior.

Now, as a grandmother, I get tickled when the younger people talk about how much work it is to have one baby. I look at them with a knowing smile and say, "Uh huh." They just hang on every word of mine. ("Yah, right, oh out-dated person of yesteryear, or so we feel at times!) I brought three adorable children, two boys and a girl, into this world. They may not always acknowledge that I am their mother, but that's beside the point. I can prove it with DNA testing. I have many wonder-ful memories of raising them with lots of love and laughter!

> Friends are gifts
> from God
> with whom we share
> our lives
> while walking
> through this world.

There seems to be a myth that we parents forget what to do when we are first time grandparents. Our minds are now mush, according to our children's perception. I still keep up my license as a nurse, and yet my oldest son, Jeff, called to me as I was chang-ing our first grandson's diaper, "Don't forget the tabs go on the Geranimal in front." Thank God he told me or I would have wrapped the baby like a taco and safety pinned the ends to the crib sheet!

Lighten up and look around at all the things you can be a part of while building relationships that can last a lifetime. Time together is often the missing ingredient. There never seems to be enough time when you're having fun with those you love.

Making Dollars or Sense

There is beauty and joy all around us every day. I have had a much greater appreciation for the simple things around me as I slow down to the speed of life that fits me better for this season of my life. I found out that speaking seven times in five days during Nurses' Week is a faster pace than my body wanted to go.

My body began to visit with me about my choices. Reflux dropped by as I stretched myself to fit my schedule and not my best interests. How much money I made during that week was not my first thought as crushing chest pain made me pause and reflect on how I had compromised my health to do just a little bit more.

Everything went well while I was "Energetically Speaking," but after everything was over, my mind still said, "Go," and my body, now thoroughly annoyed, said, "No, that's enough."

I am not afraid to die, but I do hope to have a lot of life left, as I have grandbabies to watch grow up and new friends to meet. Want to be one of my new friends? I am up to at least five now, not counting my mother, husband, or children who are "ringers" who think I'm pretty nice most of the time. Friends are gifts from God with whom we share our lives while walking through this world. They are like flowers in our life gardens, blooming where they are planted while being nourished by those around them. They also become more dear with every passing year! Friends enrich your life for more than earth's riches ever could.

There are SO many wonderful parts of life that don't cost a thing. How about watching a sunrise or sunset, taking a walk when the trees are turning colors, listening to a baby laugh, or looking into the eyes of someone you love? Enjoying the present moment with the person or people you are present with can be so fulfilling. Memories are being made in those moments and nothing can take them from you. I have heard that the only thing no one can ever take away from you is what you have become. Comedian Larry Winget once said, "Be yourself unless you are a jerk; then be someone else." My advice is to be the BEST you can be every day in every way.

Is it age or wisdom that helps us discover the joys of a simple life of contentment with significance? Age and wisdom usually go hand in hand, although, on occasion, one of them arrives alone. If you choose to be a life-long learner, you will make a great difference in this world. There is a degree of power in knowledge, but only if it is applied. Personally, I think the wisdom from things experienced gives the greater knowledge or at least the one that I remember the longest.

It is usually the odd, unique, or ridiculous experiences that we also remember the longest. Generally the things we are embarrassed about stay in our memory longer. My memory chip is almost filled with these types of things! Isn't it interesting that the embarrassing things that happen to us become the humorous stories we tell later in life.

I remember walking out to my car wearing a suit on my way to speak somewhere on a cold January day in Minnesota. When people ask why I stay in Minnesota during the winter I often respond, "Because we are the "Chosen Frozen." As I grasped the door handle on the driver's side, I slipped on the ice and slid all the way under the car with my hand still grasping the door handle. I wasn't hurt except for my pride. I started laughing as I imagined what I looked like to anyone passing by. I began thinking of what I would say if someone stopped. My first thought was a clever, "I'm just checking the oil before I leave," or "The tires look pretty good from the inside. Now I'm all set to go." You can always pretend that the mistake you made was a planned event.

* * *

Making Dollars or Sense

In the era I was raised, you were what you did. A man's or woman's identity was in his or her title and job description. One might have said, "I work at the Highway Department and am responsible for road repair." Not a good thing to share. Guess who will get all kinds of calls about where a road needs to be repaired from people who are sure you would want to know when you are at home on the weekend. Similar things happen when you are at a party and you mention that you are a nurse. People start to describe symptoms they are experiencing and show you rashes right by the chip dip! P-l-e-a-s-e!

I sat next to a woman I had never met before at a fancy banquet. She asked me to watch her during the meal and said, if suddenly she convulsed or passed out, that I should look in her purse for an injectable medication and give it to her to counteract an allergic reaction she might have to shell fish. What a relaxing meal that was! I kept watching her chew and kept looking into her eyes just

> **If you choose
> to be
> a life-long learner,
> you will make
> a great difference
> in this world.**

in case something started happening. If it did, I wanted to catch it quickly. I guess there was a speaker that evening, but I really don't recall what he said. I do remember that this woman looked like she had a good airway and great veins for an IV. Don't you just love people? You never know what to expect. There IS humor all around us but sometimes we forget to laugh.

In my parents' generation, a woman's identity was in what her husband did for a living. We called the women in our neighborhood by their married name, such as, Mrs. Jones, the banker's wife, or Mrs. Smith, the carpenter's wife. And if a woman worked outside the home, it was generally thought that she HAD to work for the money, not that she wanted to do something as well as raise a family. People in that generation would wonder WHY a woman wouldn't want to stay home. Stereotyping was rampant! Some well intentioned people actually became known for being travel agents for guilt trips when they didn't agree with your viewpoint. They felt the need to let you know so you could have the opportunity to change. Oh, how thoughtful! Thank you so very much.

Just take a guess on how the current generation would respond if someone told them their identity was embedded in someone else's occupation? Now be gentle in your thinking! Don't judge anyone, or you will get a "time out" in your room with your TV and computer games.

The jobs available for women as I was growing up (which, incidentally, I still am, as well as out), were basically as teachers, nurses, secretaries and covered wagon assistants. Which one is incorrect? There weren't any UPS women drivers, highway workers, policewomen, or women truck drivers. Nowadays, I can't think of any job a woman can't do. Well maybe Sumo wrestling, but I don't keep up with that sport so I don't really know. Women do mud wrestling - but, personally, I think they do it for facial tightness.

> Time nurtures like food, but with an expiration date as yet to be determined.

My first job was working at the old Emporium, a retail store in St. Paul, Minnesota, representing our high school on the "Teen Board." It was a real honor to be chosen to represent your high school as we modeled clothes and worked on the floor wearing the "Teen Board." uniform, which consisted of a white blouse, a red blazer with emblem, a pleated skirt and striped knee high stockings with penny loafers. A little known fact is that I was also the store's Easter bunny for one year. I wore a full bunny costume complete with a large rabbit head with ears that moved when I pulled the strings. It was my big break into show biz, passing out candy to children being trained by their parents to be future shoppers.

After I was married and had children, I used to become mildly annoyed with people who would ask me, "Do You Work?" This was at a time when I chose to stay home with three children and to work part time as a clinical nurse. I would reply tongue in cheek, "No, I stay home and watch the paint chip and the meat thaw. On really nice days I go outside and watch the grass grow and the flowers bloom." I won the District Humorous Toastmasters Competition with a presentation entitled, "Do You Work?" which was a parody on that whole issue of how people think about the importance of work. It was good for laughs and generated a lot of them because we could, and still can, relate to America's emphasis on what we do instead of who we are.

Those of us who do work outside the home need to get even more creative so we can have time to relax and enjoy our family. Remember that time nurtures like food, but with an expiration date as yet to be determined. Our lives are like a version of the old "Beat the Clock" TV show. How many things can you do before the clock stops?

I found a creative solution that saves some time and allows me to enjoy the beauty of having flowers without watering them. I have artificial flowers both indoors and out. I spray the outdoor ones with Scotchgard every so often so the water will run off them. Those of you with a green thumb are probably rolling your eyes with disbelief right now. That's good because rolling your eyes is a form of exercise. All I can say is that I have NO weeds, and my flowers, on occasion, have actually even received a compliment.

That reminds me of a time when I received a compliment when we were going out for dinner with my dear friend, Jan, from high school and her husband, Keith. She said that she really liked my hair. I paused for a moment, then quickly took the wig off my head and threw it to her saying, "Thanks...want a closer look?" She gasped, but caught it in mid air like a professional ball player! Jan has learned to expect the unexpected at all times when in my presence. We old "bats" always have a "ball" when we get together and slam down a not-so-healthy dessert occasionally. The only trouble is that our bases are getting bigger and the seats in the dugout are shrinking, probably due to rain.

Spontaneity is one sure way to increase your fun factor especially when people know that you are predisposed to spontaneous episodes of the "crazies." My precious husband, Ken, barely flinched as he watched me take off my adorable wig that night. He kept a straight face and said, "She must be off her medications again. I'll have to get her back to the home soon." Our friends solemnly nodded in agreement.

* * *

Do you find yourself comparing yourself to others and what they do? There will always

> Spontaneity is one sure way to increase your fun factor ...

be those who do more, do it better and are faster, as well as those who do less, do it worse, and are slower. I may sound like a recording, but our self worth should not be in what we DO but in who we ARE. God made Masterpieces, not junk. Our job is to discover the gifts and talents we have and use them to make a difference for a greater good.

We each have a unique purpose for being here. We need to find out what that purpose is. Find your passion by asking yourself: "What do I do that gives me a lot of satisfaction? What do I do to contribute to something that makes a difference? Who does it make a difference to? Is this something I can make a living at or is it a stepping stone as I figure out what to do with my life?"

Making Dollars or Sense

I think a lot of us didn't know enough about potential opportunities earlier in life, so it was difficult for us to know what type of career to pursue. It helps to sample different types of work by being a volunteer or shadowing someone in a position that you would consider pursuing.

Is being rich one of your life goals? What kind of riches are you looking for? There's good news if genuine wealth is what you decide you really want. The good news is that God's Word does promise riches to the believer. *Ephesians 1:18* promises that we will know what is the hope of His calling, what are the riches of the glory of His inheritance. With that inheritance, we also get: (1) An understanding of God the Father and the Son, "in whom are hidden all the treasures of wisdom and knowledge" *(Colossians 2:2-3)*. (2) Contentment. "I am not saying this because I am in need, for I have learned to be content whatever the circumstances. I know what it is to be in need, and I know what it is to have plenty. I can do everything through him who gives me strength *(Philippians 4:11-13)*. (3) All our needs are met by God *(Philippians 4:19)*.

God's word promises us great riches - treasures like eternal life that we cannot even attempt to purchase with any amount of money. It has already been paid for in full on the cross. Our job is to humbly accept this incredible gift. Some of us feel that we have to earn everything - that there is no free lunch!" But we are not saved by our works *(Ephesians 2:8-9)*.

Eternal life is the banquet that has been prepared for us. The price was more than you or I could ever afford but is offered as a free gift to those who believe and accept Jesus as their Lord and Savior *(John 1:12)*.

* * *

Do you think you have enough? "Enough of what?" you may ask. Good question. My answer is: "Enough of everything you think you need to exist here on earth, in the lifestyle you choose, for as long as you expect to live. Take your best guess, remembering that your health is truly your wealth, especially if living long and living well appeal to you.

How much IS enough, and will it ever be enough? Do we expect God to supply as much as we want or as much as we need? *"Your Father knows the things you have need of before you ask Him. Therefore do not worry, saying, 'What shall we eat? Or what shall we drink? Or what shall we wear?'"* (Matthew 6:8, 31) God provides for us from the fullness of His love. That works for me. HE knows how long we will be here so that takes care of the guessing on our part, as we, instead, ask for wisdom and discernment each day to make good decisions according to His will for our lives.

I personally need to remember to stop "asking" and start "thanking!" We just can't out give God. If you think you have given too much at church or have helped others too much, don't worry. God is honest. If you give too much, He will give it back! Your reward may be in good health, more true friends who are there for you and other ways that cannot be measured in dollars but make a lot of sense.

1 Timothy 6: 17-18 cautions us not to put our hope in wealth, which is so uncertain, but to put our hope in God who richly provides us with everything for our enjoyment. Be rich in good deeds and be generous and willing to share. Take hold of the life that is truly life. *1 Timothy 6:6* says, *"Godliness with contentment is great gain."*

* * *

I have learned that making a living is not the same as making a life. Let me explain. I have realized that the things I have because of income are basically tangible. The things that make my life really worth living are not tangible. When you understand this principle and it really sinks in, it is so freeing! Most of us have seen pictures or movies showing children living in poverty with smiles on their faces playing with a can or a piece of string. Why did it take so long to figure out that living a life that matters rather than one that impresses others is much more fulfilling?

I truly am not some prude who doesn't enjoy having a comfortable home and driving a car that feels good to my aging body that turned out not to be wrinkle proof. I knew I should have read the warranty clause. Oh well…when in doubt and want to shout…just sing out loud and attract a crowd. How do I know that? Ah, the myth of staying young. What a game we play as we wrinkle away. That could be a song. I remember breaking into a song while my children were around. They would quickly ask, "Mother, who sings that song?" I would then name the artist, and they would respond, "Let them."

> **I have learned that making a living is not the same as making a life.**

Nice things are nice but often not necessary. If we start to learn to live with less we will not be so shocked when disasters happen, and we are inconvenienced, deprived, or devastated.

* * *

So much of who we are begins in how we think. *"As a man thinketh, so is he" (Proverbs 23:7).* Pastor and author A.W. Tozer said: "Our voluntary thoughts not only reveal what we are, they predict what we will become."

What do you want to become? More importantly, who do you want to become? What qualities do you want to demonstrate in your life? I have found that I am finally choosing to care less about what I do, and to care more about who I am in God's eyes. Just a few moments ago, while listening to our local Christian Radio Station, KTIS, a popular Christian recording artist, Christy

I Only Have a Minute ... So Let's Make It Matter!

Nochols, said that she and her husband were choosing to stop doing concerts requiring them to be on the road. They decided that being home with their children was far more important. A comment she made was so timely for me as I write this book. She said, "Don't love what you DO more than you love God." She and her husband went on to explain that in their later years they would probably not be talking about that huge concert in Tampa but about the memories they made with their family because they were there with them.

Deciding what matters to you is totally individual. Do you want to make dollars and lots of them (new boat, here I come), OR do you want to make "sense" (come here and tell me what's wrong…I am here for you) along with the number of dollars that will meet your real needs?

I am thinking that real needs are those necessary for survival. Perceived needs may be what you think you need, like a microwave or a cell phone, but are really a convenience. I feel so spoiled when I look around at what I used to think seemed so important, and that I could easily have gone without. Unfortunately, our base line for what we think we really need to survive keeps getting longer as more conveniences become available.

This chapter is meant to be thought provoking. Are the reasons for doing what you do legitimate for meeting the outcomes you value or desire? What are you leaving on earth that will live on? Our children are living legacies of our love. May the light of God's everlasting love shine from you and through you to others as you seek to find the true value of a life lived in service to others. Fill yourself with knowledge and wisdom while learning to love yourself unconditionally just as God loves you right this very minute. Life was His gift to you. What you do with it is your gift back to Him. Be generous.

Chapter Three

Living Love

"Those who bring sunshine to the lives of others cannot keep it from themselves." There is a lot of truth in that! I'd like to say I was the author of that quote, but in honesty, it belongs to James Barrie, author of Peter Pan. Sounds like a "fly by night" to me.

You get what you give is another way of explaining that principle. We need to practice living positively on purpose. When you smile at someone, they will often smile back or some may even scowl as they wonder what you have been up to or what you want. When you live love, you get love. Unhappy people are the ones who need love the most but are probably the least likely to receive it because of their outward demeanor and actions.

What does living love really mean or what does it look like to others? To seven-year-old Bobby, it looks like this: "Love is what's in the room with you at Christmas if you stop opening presents and listen." What does the verb "living" love conjure up in your mind? In my mind, which has limited seating, I see people helping others without having an agenda for themselves or what they will receive by doing whatever it is they do.

Their act of kindness, whatever it may be, is not self serving. Rather, it is a way of allowing God to express His love to others through you. It means freely undertaking a task or commit ment necessary to help another's emotional, physical, or spiritual well being.

I was recently allowed the privilege of providing a small act of kindness that blessed me beyond belief in the process. As I was leaving our local health clinic, I saw a grandmother carrying a baby accompanied by two teenage girls. I stopped, smiled and asked how old their adorable baby was. They told me, with big smiles on their faces as I acknowledged their precious child. I smiled and headed for my van. As I started to drive away, I heard the grandma calling out to me, "Lady, lady." I saw her in the rearview mirror running after my van. I pulled over, stopped, opened the door and called back to her. "Are you OK?"

> When we do these things, we make God's love tangible. It is like giving our prayers 'legs.'

"Yes," she said. "I just wondered if you would give us a ride just over to Valley Creek Road." Oh, of course, I would be happy to give you all a ride. It's very warm out and that is quite a walk.

They explained that they were dropped off but had no way to get home except to walk. The grandmother kept thanking me as we drove. I told her to thank God because He knew their needs and I just showed up to carry out His will. Oh, I know she said ... He takes care of us! When I dropped them off the grandma told me her name, asked for mine and then asked if she could pray for me and my family, which I readily agreed to, before I left. I told this dear lady that she had blessed me much more than I blessed them. We agreed that we would meet again, at least ultimately in our Father's house. She smiled and waved as I drove away with a joy in my heart feeling so blessed to have had the privilege of serving my Savior with this small act of kindness. That very morning in my prayer time I had asked God to let me give "a cup of cold water" to someone that day. He not only answered my prayer with a *"yes,"* but He flavored the water with the sweet taste of His faithfulness.

When we do these things we make God's love tangible. It is like giving our prayers "legs." Our compassion is in action. We are doing something about circumstances that need attention, but we do not expect anything in return. It does take time, but that becomes part of the gift we give. Our time is well invested with dividends that are out of this world!

In order to serve others in this way, we need to be secure in our identity of having great worth and value. Those being served will hopefully realize the inner joy we receive from this outward expression of inner abundance.

Helping family members is a great way to get immediately involved when a need develops, because usually you are one of the first to know about it. I really believe that being a care giver is a calling. Sometimes it sounds more like a holler or a scream. We, the people here on earth, at one time or another, will almost all need to be cared for by someone who cares enough to do it, either paid or unpaid.

My background in nursing has helped me to understand the satisfaction that comes from the unspoken expressions that come after the care is completed. It is different, however, knowing that you can go to your own home when your shift is over. You can then have some down time to rejuvenate your tired body as well as your tired mind from the physical and the emotional strain that often accompanies the task of caring for others. Compassion fatigue is common for those who care for others on a regular basis.

I learned a very significant life lesson about care-giving when I was on the "other" side of the bed and my husband became my care giver. I started to experience sporadic back pain accompanied by leg pain and jerking muscles which I tried to convince myself was from over exercising, but I knew better! Trust me on that one. After a number of tests, I found out that I had degenerative disks that were hereditary. The doctor kept saying my condition would require a "really big surgery." That meant PAIN to me, but I figured pain is relative to where you are on a scale of one to ten. Living with chronic pain sounded worse to me than one BIG "owie" (medical term for those of you not in the health care field), especially if the surgery would solve the pain problem.

An anterior-posterior spinal fusion was performed to an un-applauding audience, using four screws to hold my "still young but acting very old" disks together. My spine was crooked from birth and it did not close at the bottom, which is called a benign spina bifida. The surgeons had to enter my body from the front and the back to obtain a solid fusion. All of the organs in my pelvis were reorganized. One of the surgeons made a 13-inch incision in the front, moved my organs (which were not playing a tune at the time) over while they inserted four screws to fuse my L4 and L5.

Now that's probably more than you wanted to know, but there's more! They then flipped me over, made another incision so they could pack bone taken from my hip around my spine. I wore a molded brace for three months, which I only took off for showers and sleeping at night. I resembled a bionic woman as I rapped on my stomach and said: "Me woman, hear me whine."

Stereotypes of how husbands typically care for their wives caused me to keep my expectations of Ken's ability to care for me quite low. Given my situation, anything more than meeting basic needs would be pretty extraordinary, as I looked at it.

Living Love

My dear husband, however, is this logical, precise, quiet type of guy who turned into Superman. When I would wake up at 2 AM in extreme pain, he would quickly ask, "What do you need? Hot packs? Cold packs? Medication? Pillows? Wow! Without even going into a phone booth, Ken was transformed into my "Super Hero" without leotards. Thank God, because the visual on that would not be good.

My orthopedic surgeon said I was the fastest healing patient he had had in the last fifteen years after having surgery of that magnitude. I attribute a lot of the credit to Ken with his positive, you can do it…and I will help you 'til you can, attitude. Ken would take me to our local health club. I wore my molded brace lashed over my swim suit which was quite a fashion statement. This was not the perfect Ken and Barbie picture, let me tell you! I looked like I was still strapped in a box with the largest curve being my butt. I walked using small steps trying not to jar my freshly healing insides that were ticked off from all the redecorating inside! Ken would brace himself against me as he supported me going down the steps into the whirlpool. He would then walk me around in a circle so I could move my muscles while letting the warm water soothe my damaged back porch. He called me his little "duck butt." I must have quacked him up.

I couldn't dress myself from the waist down from June 23 until August 4 that year, when the strong-willed child within me finally said, "Today I'm dressing myself alone." Ken asked if I needed some assistance, but I was determined. I used the clamp on my curling iron and my spaghetti tongs to pull on my undergarment, slacks, and even those funny short nylons that look so cute when you push them down to your ankles, or when they fall down as you shake your leg. I used to do that to entertain my children when they were teenagers. My daughter would look at whoever else was in the room and say, "I'm adopted."

I Only Have a Minute ... So Let's Make It Matter!

Ken never complained about having to care for me, as far as I know. I asked him how he would feel if he would have to dress and care for me the rest of my life. He said it would affect our lifestyle, but that it wasn't all that bad. We really can adapt to what life brings our way. The difficult things of life build our character while making us even more grateful for simple pleasures that we now may take for granted, like being able to bend over and clip our toe nails. I know that's not a "big thing," but it is if your feet are "pointie" and rip your husband's leg at night. You get the point. Actually they do if you don't keep trimming the little hummers.

> Some transparency
> is needed
> to really connect
> with others.

During the Christmas season that year, six months after my surgery, I remember walking through a mall with Ken. Suddenly I stopped, looked at Ken with the biggest smile and said, "I don't hurt ANYWHERE!" What a profound and precious gift I received in that moment of realization. How thankful I am to be married to a man who loves and cares for me just as I am, or, as they say on discount racks, "As Is!" *I Thessalonians 1:3* says it so well: *"Our labor is prompted by love, and our endurance is inspired by hope."*

After that experience, whenever I presented before an audience, I would wear a chain around my neck with a key from an electric cart that I once rode as a sign of humility. None of us knows from one moment to the next when we might be the one who needs to be cared for. The care I received has given me an even greater sense of joy when I assist others doing whatever I can to give them the relief I so gratefully received.

My relationship with my husband deepened after that experience, as our appreciation for one another grew even greater.

Living Love

We don't take our health for granted knowing, from experience, how quickly things can change. A true gift to someone you care about is time spent together doing little things that show you care. Love should be a lifestyle. Don't wait for a major life event or a holiday to do kind and thoughtful things for those special people in your life.

Jessica, age 8, said it well: "You really shouldn't say, 'I love you,' unless you mean it. But if you mean it, you should say it a lot. People forget." Relationships at every level, from a hello to a hug, are what ground us and give our lives meaning

You limit the quality of your life if you limp along as a lone ranger with many nice acquaintances but few, if any, people who really know you well. Do you remember the song, *People*? It says people who need people are the luckiest people in the world. Drugs, alcohol and food can't give you a hug. They are just "Band-Aids" that mask, for only moments, what you really need. What we really NEED is other people to stimulate our senses in a positive way.

I know the analytical types reading this are probably shaking their heads, thinking, "I knew it, this is one of those touchy, feely books." Well, here's a thought from the heart…real men DO cry and DO show they care. Real women love and adore real men. Underneath the exteriors we show to the world, we have this interior that is wonderfully complicated, yet basically simple when our one driving need is to love and to be loved.

Some transparency is needed to really connect with others. We need to be able to relate and identify with others in their celebrations and when their heart is breaking. Our desire for genuine relationships helps us to open up and go deeper with others so they can get to know us better. I know that building relationships is not time efficient in a high tech world because meaningful relationships take time and a commitment to nurture and be there no matter what time it is or how inconvenient. However, you do reap what you sow or, in other words, you get what you give to others. Isn't it an interesting paradox that you have more when you give more away? This is one of the important reasons I wanted to write this book.

Here is something to remember about relationships: they take time to build, but can be damaged in a moment. So guard your moments ... and your tongue. Speaking without thinking can lead to war in our relationships.

> When we switch our focus from ourselves and our needs to others and their needs, exciting things often happen.

If you are questioning whether to say a certain thing or not, there is a general rule: When in doubt, don't. If you ever wonder whether a certain comment may offend someone, follow the rule, "When in doubt, leave it out." Sensitivity to other's feelings is a critical piece in building a relationship that will last.

You may have heard the saying, "You can forget what someone said and you can forget what they did, but you can never forget how they made you feel." Your assignment for today is to make someone else feel important, loved, and cared about.

Thinking before you speak is a wonderful skill, but it is hard to do. Ask yourself if what you are about to say is uplifting, encouraging, or helpful without being critical or self serving. If it does not meet that criteria learn how to keep your mouth sealed until some kind thought comes along. This can be tricky. Note: duct tape does not go with every outfit. My son-in-law gave me a t-shirt for my birthday that said, "I'm talking and I can't shut up." Oh the grief I bear.

When we switch our focus from ourselves and our needs to others and their needs, exciting things often happen. After my father died a couple of years, ago my mother had some anxiety, on occasion, which affected her blood pressure. The doctor, after examining her, gave her the following prescription: "Go and read to the blind." He then followed up by saying she would improve when she stopped looking inward and started living outward.

That may have sounded a bit harsh, but it worked. My mother took the theory of his advice by starting to look around to see what others around her might like or need. She delighted in bringing bananas to other seniors who couldn't get out. She also found joy in bringing treats to the den area where she lives to share with others. When we bring joy to others, it lights up our world as well!

I like to envision people looking for ways to help those who cannot or do not know how to help themselves. Knowing who needs help is something you sense when you see someone in need. Your head and heart join forces as you focus on the task at hand. Watch for the look of disbelief on the face of the one needing a hand and you show up. Unfortunately, people often become suspicious of others who want to give of themselves in the pure interest of helping another person without even knowing them. When they ask you why you want to help, you could spew forth great words of wisdom such as, "many hands make light work," or "two hands are better than one.' These sayings come in "handy." (Oh, pleeese…) Hey, it is my book.

Don't forget to let the child within you come out and play. I just did, even though it was a very short recess. If you are fun to be around, you will attract others looking for friends. Humor connects people in a delightful way. Conclusion: I think humor helps most everything. For further evidence, read other books on the subject. My book isn't the only one. I am open-minded. In fact, I am so open-minded, there is almost a draft at times. We are all better together, especially when we laugh! Go ahead. Try it right now. I am virtually laughing with you in my heart. Feel better? However, I heard that the only Book you will ever read where the Author *really is* there with you when you read it is the Bible.

* * *

Have you noticed that our world seems to be getting a lot less caring? Our safety is being compromised all over the world. Poverty and anger have bred desperation and violence. In my mind, CNN stands for "constantly negative news." Zig Zigler said, "I read the newspaper and the Bible everyday because I want to know what both sides are up to." Good point and practice. We need to dwell, however, on what is going right...and then go with it. Our mindset impacts our behavior.

Look for the good in everyone. Affirm them for what they are doing right. Human nature, however, tends to believe that you "help" others when you tell them what they are doing wrong and what needs improvement. It is like being a mother who wants everything about her child to be perfect. You hear, "Zip up your zipper, put on your mittens," and then she scrubs the child's face with a Kleenex she just spit on. As a parting farewell you hear, "And don't get hit by a car," as if that were the child's goal for the day. People who are perfectionists, like this mom, are usually critical. Critical people are often angry inside themselves. We will never be perfect in this world so there will be times of frustration, feeling you just don't measure up when you are around these people. Choose to be around these people only when you need to be.

Unfortunately, we often become like the people we are around, or we take on a trait or two of theirs, so beware and be wise. If you own a business, hire the happy. They are more fun to work with.

Showing you care about others is made apparent in the way you listen to them. When people really listen to each other, they rarely argue. When you care about what someone is saying you don't interrupt them, but focus totally on them and the message they are relating. Lean forward, look into their eyes (they are windows to their soul), be open to receive what they are saying, and show empathy. As Dr. Lyman K. (Manny) Steil, Chairman and CEO of the International Listening Institute says, "The end result of great listening is to take meaningful action. Anything less is just an interesting exercise." Do something that matters based on what you just heard. You can learn something from everyone you meet if you really listen to them. Ask a question or clarify a point when others are sharing, so you feel more involved and so they know that you really do care.

> 'The end result of great listening is to take meaningful action. Anything less is just an interesting exercise.'
> - Dr. Lyman Steil

You could also clarify what they said by saying something like, "It is my understanding you now want to purchase 1,000 of my books because you are so impressed with the information on the front and back cover? I can understand that, but wait until you read the words inside. What? You have and it changed your life forever? You are now happier than you have ever been in your whole life with a NEW outlook, a better marriage, happier children, and a greater appreciation for what you DO with your brief time here on earth?" OK ... as I said before, this is my book. I am in my own world, and the people know me there.

Moving right along to another important point as we learn to live and walk in love. We need to dwell on our strengths, not in a self centered way but in an "I can do that" type of self talk. *"I can do all things through Christ who strengthens me." (Philippians 4:13.)* Every time I present, I say to myself before going onstage, *"Be anxious for nothing. Abide in me and in my words and I will give you the desires of your heart."* (See *John 15:7*.) I feel an energized peace knowing that I am there to serve and not to shine. My job is to look out there ... and CARE!

When I was in Toastmasters, one of the popular mind management techniques to overcome the number one fear of people, which is public speaking, was to visualize everyone in the audience as being naked. I pondered that comment, and then thought to myself that this wouldn't help me at all because doing so would simply make me think I was at work as a nurse! Choosing how we think begins with an awareness of how much of a difference it makes to choose our thoughts. What we repeat and believe tends to shape what we become, and in belief there is power!

> We judge others by our perceptions and their actions. We judge ourselves by our intentions

We actually choose how happy we are going to be every day. God gives us a well-spring of joy that fills every part of our lives if we are willing to embrace it and acknowledge where it really comes from. When life isn't all about US, we are a lot more relaxing and fun to be around because we don't have to prove our worth and our value every time we open our mouths.

Taking our eyes off ourselves helps us focus on bringing joy and happiness to others. This is not a natural thing to do, but God never called us to a natural lifestyle. I worked with seniors for a number of years in a variety of capacities. They are, in general, very appreciative for everything you do for them. You get big smiles, lots of hugs, and warm looks as you perform simple acts of kindness for them. I got paid every two weeks as a nurse, but every time I worked I received an emotional check that no one else could cash.

Living Love

When I was working the relief shift one evening, an elderly lady asked me if I would have time to give her a hug. She was lying in bed and I was about to give her medications. I looked at her warm smile and quickly said, "Of course." As I put the medications aside, I realized that I was going to administer a much more important alternative medicine...the power of a hug! She snuggled down in her bed, looked up at me with warm, caring eyes that twinkled and said, "I like you. Are you going to work tomorrow?" I just got paid.

* * *

Did you know that our work should be a celebration of who we are? Can people tell that you are celebrating when they see you at work, or does your body say, "Caffeine – then words!"

Our body language also speaks loudly to those around us. Stand tall, walk tall and look carefully with a smile at those around you. We need to be aware of the type of environment that is being created by our body language. Do we look rushed and harried or does our demeanor say, "Life is good and I'm OK? How are you?"

I remember, after working in an emergency room setting, taking a long-term care nursing position. As I hurried down the hall in what I thought was an efficient, professional manner, an elderly woman stopped me and said, "Slow down honey, you're making me nervous." What I thought was efficient was perceived as annoying to others! How could that be? That incident taught me a lot. We judge others by our perceptions and their actions. We judge ourselves by our intentions. Creating a positive emotional environment where we work makes a huge difference in the way our customers perceive the service they receive. That goes back to how we make others feel.

I Only Have a Minute ... So Let's Make It Matter!

When hiring people who would be serving others, I found that hiring those who genuinely cared about others was a much better hiring decision than employing more experienced workers who didn't seem to care. You can teach technical skills to people, but you cannot teach them to care. To be genuinely concerned about other people requires an attitude of respect as well as an unconditional positive regard for all those you meet, with no exceptions.

I found some great examples of this concept in a great book I was reading. It is filled with timely wisdom and makes the point a lot better than I do, so I would like to share the following truths with you from that great book, better known as the Bible.

Romans 12:9-16: "Love must be sincere. Hate what is evil; cling to what is good. Be devoted to one another in brotherly love. Honor one another above yourselves. Never be lacking in zeal, but keep your spiritual fervor, serving the Lord. Be joyful in hope, patient in affliction and faithful in prayer. Share with God's people who are in need. Practice hospitality. Bless those who persecute you; bless and do not curse. Rejoice with those who rejoice; mourn with those who mourn. Live in harmony with one another. Do not be proud, but be willing to associate with people of low position. Do not be conceited."

When you give to others, the condition of your heart is revealed. Giving is an expression of gratitude for everything you have been blessed with. It is a tangible way of saying thank you to God, whom you cannot "out give!" Giving connects us to the world and opens our eyes to the needs of others. I see how vast the need, how short the time, and how unimportant most of my stuff is by comparison. The things of this world do grow strangely dim in the light of HIS glory and grace!

When we become content with what we have, we become more useful for greater things. Pride and arrogance get washed away. Giving has opened my eyes to who I am and shows my body, mind, and spirit that I have more than enough. I have what I really need and I am thankful! I am the caretaker of my resources. *"Your labor is prompted by love and your endurance inspired by hope in our Lord, Jesus Christ." (1 Thessalonians 1:3)*

This love that God talks about doesn't seek a return on its investment: It is not self-seeking (see *1 Corinthians 13:5*). Caring for someone expecting they will care for us in return is simply an indirect means of controlling someone else.

> When we become content with what we have, we become more useful for greater things.

I've found that people who try to control others do not feel loved. They feel that if they stopped manipulating people they would be abandoned. They have a deep fear of isolation. *"There is no fear in real love. Perfect love drives out fear." (1 John 4:18)*. The lesson to be learned is that we cannot manipulate or make others feel guilty and expect to be loved by them at the same time.

One of my favorite writers, ANON, said it well: "True love is when you love someone more than you need them." That is so true from what I have observed in life. My husband and I laugh a lot when we are together. We genuinely enjoy each other's company, even if we are just sitting in a room together doing something independently ... me flossing my teeth and Ken cleaning out his ears. He is much more reserved than I am, but so is Bozo the clown. I can't count on him, however, to make me happy. None of us can count on others to make our lives purposeful and fulfilling. That is up to us, working from the inside out, starting with our heart and soul. Joy that lasts comes from within.

I Only Have a Minute ... So Let's Make It Matter!

I am learning not to expect anything from others, which really sets me and them free. It is not out of being negative, just realistic. I am admitting that I don't have or need control over others. If family or friends stop by or call, that is great; but if they don't, I'm still OK. Learning to be alone with ourselves without outside stimuli is a wonderful skill to learn.

Being alone can help develop inner peace with or without aroma-therapy and water drizzling over some rocks. We need to love ourselves before we can honestly love others so they can fully feel our sincere love for them because we know how that feels.

In order to give to others fully we need to come from a place of abundance, especially abundant thinking. Abundant thinking comes when you have a positive outlook, and an inner spirit that looks for the good in every situation. Furthermore, we need to surround ourselves with people who come from a place of abundance to recharge ourselves. *"As iron sharpens iron, so one man sharpens another." (Proverbs 27:17)* We often become like the people we are around so choose the friends you want to spend more time with wisely.

A corollary to that was spoken by Dale Carnegie: "We tend to like the people who like us." He added, "The best way to interest others in us is to take an interest in them." That is REALLY true! How many of us like visiting with, or more appropriately, listening to, someone just talk about themselves? Someone who never asks the listener questions about themselves is being rude. Good communication is like a game of ping pong. There must be an exchange of conversation to keep things stimulating for both parties. Besides that...talking to yourself looks tacky and you all ready know the information so why bother?

Conversation is really a life skill to be continually improved upon over your lifetime. There is usually something we can learn from almost every conversation. Whom do you admire as a great conversationalist? Model what you see and practice what you hear.

* * *

We need a customer service mentality in our relationships. Make enthusiasm a way of life. Be contagious. It is harder to be enthusiastic when you're tired, broke, or bored, so get enough rest, work hard, and be a life long learner. Don't catch other people's lack of enthusiasm. A straight face with no expression doesn't make a very pretty picture. A smile, however, can light up a room with positive energy that says "I like you. Let's get to know one another."

> **You can transform a drab existence into a dazzling adventure if you believe you can.**

Life is a self fulfilling prophecy. There is power in believing. You can transform a drab existence into a dazzling adventure if you believe you can. As we grow older we will inevitably have loss, loneliness, illness and incapacity. Nonetheless, give yourself regular mental pep talks. Say: "I'm strong, capable, happy, beautiful, energetic, successful and smart." What you repeat and believe tends to shape what you become, and in belief there is power. Find work you enjoy, nurture old and new friendships, help others, and have FUN along the way! He who laughs lasts. They also keep their jobs longer and have friendships that last a lifetime.

A wise man once said, "You may not always get what you want, but you will usually get what you expect, so expect the BEST!" Attract abundance… *"As a man thinketh so is he." (Proverbs 23:7.)* That goeth for women too! Author Elizabeth O'Connor, well-known for her book *Journey Inward, Journey Outward* said, "Envy is a symptom of lack of appreciation of our own uniqueness and self worth. Each of us has something to give that no one else has." We have permission to discover ourselves as we submerge ourselves in knowledge which becomes applied wisdom when we do something with it. We multiply our strengths through our friends and acquaintances when we share common goals. Visionary thinking with positive outcomes that are bigger than ourselves create energy which generates action.

It does take time and commitment to nurture friendships, but it is one of the single best investments that you will ever make. We are wired to connect. The purpose or object of life is to give life to others. Nido Qubein said, "We are as rich as our relationships." Make your commitments carefully as changing your mind later often means that you didn't do your homework up front. Ready, Set, Think, Learn, Reflect, Go! Change is the engine of growth, so don't be afraid to try new things, go new places, and make new friends.

T.E. Kemps: "It is futile to wish for a long life, and then to give so little care to living well." Well said! It isn't the quantity or length of your life that is as important as the quality of your existence. Quality can be measured in how many people love you and you love in return. Being healthy also helps. Your health is your wealth so why not get rich?

> 'It is futile to wish for a long life, and then to give so little care to living well.'
> - T.E. Kemps

Love manifests itself best in relationships ... the caring, committed connection of one individual to another. We need to be connected. We need people to bond with, trust, and go to for support and encouragement. We are built, from the beginning, for relationships and attachments. Babies need a consistent, warm, loving and predictable emotional environment to be healthy and feel secure. So do we. We swaddle babies and we hug everyone else to both nurture and show our affection. Demonstrating our feelings is very important when it comes to growing our relationships, which hopefully are a priority in our lives. Tell people that you care about them, and then show them that you do with small acts of thoughtfulness whenever an opportunity arises.

Your Day Planner is often what dictates the priorities in your life. What you believe in, you make time for. You may need to schedule times of relaxation for yourself and with others. One way may be to make a list of who you would like to spend more time with and then call them on the telephone to make your mutual desires happen.

> **We are wired to connect. The purpose or object of life is to give life to others.**

How wonderful it is these days to receive telephone calls instead of emails! It is a sign of the times that many people send off a quick email rather than call you on the telephone when both parties are equally available. Decide what is more important. Is it the time you save or the possibility of building a more meaningful relationship? It may be a small brick in the building of the relationship but the warmth of your voice along with "you are worth my time to call" makes a statement that a quick email never will. We are losing our interpersonal communication skills the more we use and depend on our electronic friends who we know can forget about us in a "click." If you have ever felt or have actually been deleted from someone's life, you realize the importance of real people verses equipment that may misinterpret your true message and not really care.

Communicating with others in a variety of ways keeps your creative juices flowing. I have been known to leave clever notes in strange places to surprise my husband who looks amused when he finds them. Consciousness is that annoying time between naps, so we might as well have fun while we are awake!

In my observations of life I have noticed that, on occasion, people will love things and use people. It should be the other way around. We should love people and use things. Now, it's true, many of the things we love mean something about someone we love, such as a glass dish that grandma put cookies on for the grandchildren whenever they came over or a favorite book that was read to them by their grandpa. The meaning or significance of the "thing" is due to the memories of the special people in their lives attached to it. Think about fun ways to make memories that leave a legacy. Encourage elders to tell their stories regarding their life's accomplishments. Brainstorm with your family about things they would like to do with you. Make a list and then make a plan as to where and when you will enjoy some special time together. Be considerate of other people's finances so you don't embarrass them if they cannot afford what others want to do. It doesn't have to be costly. A picnic in a park by a public swimming place is something everyone can enjoy. Walking or biking on public trails can be an adventure as well as a great time to catch up on each other's lives.

> **Think about
> fun ways
> to make memories
> that leave a legacy.**

Other "things" that we love are definitely wants and not needs. Don't be sad about the things you want and don't get. Think how many things you **don't** want that you **don't** get! Now that is one way to remain more thankful.

Some people live love by expressing contentment with their present condition in life, whatever it may be. I was talking with a very interesting woman in her sixties who works with developmentally challenged people. She said that every morning she looks in the mirror and says, "I am beautiful and everyone loves me." She repeats that a few times and claims that before long she is feeling good about herself.

After she had shared that wonderful bit of wisdom, she paused and added, "I am not a woman of means, you know, and I live in a small trailer. Every day I also tell myself that my home is just perfect for me. I repeat that a few times, and my home does start looking better to me. I leave for work thinking of how blessed I am to be alive, live near my daughter, and feel good physically, mentally and spiritually. A happy tune comes to mind as I head out the door now humming a little ditty about being pretty."

What a blessing that advice was to me! She not only accepted her life situation, which sounded very satisfactory, but she also helped herself and those around her have a better day because she passed their way sporting a more positive outlook.

* * *

I wanted to leave this chapter with LOVE, so I have one more significant story to share with you about the power of love in our family as it continued to reveal itself in ways we could never have imagined.

My precious daughter, Julie, having lost three children felt a great need to continue her journey to become a mother. She became pregnant with twins and after six months, with Julie's history, Dr. Drake and Dr. Mahone decided to put her on bed rest in the hospital so they could keep a close watch. In the middle of that first week, while having a sonogram, the heartbeat of one of the babies stopped. Grief came to visit once again. There was no apparent reason for the sudden death of this baby according to the doctors, who shared our grief and our renewed concern for the other living twin.

I Only Have a Minute ... So Let's Make It Matter!

We decided to bring Christmas to Julie in Iowa that year because we knew she couldn't travel and be away from her doctors in case anything else happened. My other two sons and their families traveled to Iowa, as well. We stayed at a hotel, opened Christmas gifts the night before Christmas Eve because Julie had more signs that things could be starting to happen. She wasn't due until March, so this was another potentially dangerous situation.

John was to meet us in church the next morning and then we were to go back to their home for brunch. John never showed up. We found out later that while we were at church, John and Julie were speeding to the hospital with hard contractions, many tears, and two faithful hearts pleading with God to let this baby live.

When we got to the car after church, I immediately called their home and, of course, no one answered. We headed for the hospital, a lump in our throats and prayers on our lips. Please Lord, don't let the unthinkable happen again!!

The doctors had started IV medication to stop the contractions. Julie reassured us that all would be fine. She said we should return about 3 p.m. for a nice visit after things quieted down. After lunch my heart began to race and the "mother in me" sensed that something was happening with Julie. Call it intuition if you like. I call it "mother radar". We just know. So I called John on his cell phone, and, again, no one answered. I then called the hospital room, not ready to give up my quest for information. After all, I am a type A mother with an inquiring mind that wants to know. John answered the phone in Julie's room hurriedly saying, "We are going into delivery!" and he hung up. Off we headed toward an unknown outcome with great expectations that God was going to give our family a well-deserved miracle after already taking back four precious babies.

Living Love

The nurse came out saying Julie was presently delivering the stillborn. We waited, praying with every breath. The nurse came out with tears of joy trickling down her face. She said, "I have never wanted a baby to live more ... he's alive and headed to intensive care right now."

John came out to share that he was the proud father of a two-pound, five-ounce son, Samuel John. We were allowed to join him in the Intensive Care unit where we met our miracle grandson. As I walked into the unit the nurse looked at me crying and asked, "Grandmother?" I said, "Yes!" and then I moved over to take a closer look at our dear Samuel.

Another miracle was about to happen. John put his hand alongside Sam in his incubator. This tiny baby, one half hour old reached over and wrapped his little hand around his daddy's finger as a sign to all of us that you could almost feel him say, "Hey dad, I'm going to live. I'm going to make it." God remained faithful. As I write this book, Sam is now four years old! When we were at their home about a year ago, Sam came into our bedroom in the early morning, walked right in and said, with prompting from his father, "Get up old people!" I looked at my husband and said, "That would be us, we'd better get up!" Laughter rang in a celebration of love as we laughed with life together. The fact that Sam is alive is reason enough to celebrate!

One of the observations I made while visiting little Sammy in the hospital during the months following his birth was the loving care administered freely to our miracle baby by all the staff. On the lower half of the crib, the nurses placed a sign that read, "Love Is How I Grow." That was everyone's job – to help Sammy grow. Life was indeed bittersweet with the loss of Jacob, Sammy's twin brother, and then the joy of having this precious first live child of John and Julie finally in our arms.

I Only Have a Minute ... So Let's Make It Matter!

My daughter has a strong faith along with the gift of creativity. She found THE perfect birth announcement which we have framed sitting on a special shelf surrounded by porcelain angels. The bottom part of the announcement has the picture of two beautiful angel babies. The verse above them reads:

Every good and perfect gift is from above,
We were blessed with twins to cherish and love,
Born together to grow apart,
One in our hands, one in our heart.

Born 12 ½ weeks early on December 23, 2001
Into God's Hands:
Jacob Wesley
Stillborn

Into Our Hands;
Samuel John
2 pounds, 5 ounces
14 inches
3:38 PM

[The parents' names]

We will always keep this announcement visibly displayed and indelibly printed forever in our hearts.

The message to remember is:

Love Is How We ALL Grow

Go in Love, and Be Sure to Share It With Others.
You Will Grow, and So Will They!

Chapter Four

Is Busy Better?

Ask anyone what they have been up to lately and they will almost always say, "Busy, I've been busy." The other statement heard quite often, especially from senior citizens, is "keeping busy," as if being busy is an important goal. Are you better because you are busy? As we take time to reflect on the quality, not the quantity, of our lives, we can't help but wonder if being busy is really better. "Better than what?" you might ask. "Beware of the barrenness of a busy life" (Socrates). He apparently thought being busy was not better, and I agree.

For WHAT are we striving for which we must go faster in order to obtain? I sometimes think (which is a good thing to do occasionally ... it scares your brain into action ...) that some of us may be addicted to the adrenaline rush we get while multi-tasking. Do we love the result of our efforts or the act of getting many things done, thus proving our worth and value? Are we more valuable because we do more? More of what? Is it the "what" that gives value, or is it in the "doing?"

A short time ago I was in a plane observing fellow passengers "doing," as we all waited for the plane to take off. Then I heard the airline steward say, "Please end your telephone conversations, as we will be taking off soon." Welcome to the world of modern technology! Put that on your blog. I am not a technology nut ... well, part of that statement is true, but I'll let you figure out which one. Technology does save us time, once we learn how to use it effectively. But the time saved is often consumed exploring all the capabilities of technology, which will never end because technology is in a constant state of change.

The vast amount of information technology puts at your fingertips can become frustrating because you don't have time to learn all you'd like to know, you hungry mind you, so you don't get some of the tasks done that were more important to accomplish. It's like eating a bag of sour cream and onion potato chips. You can't eat just one.

> **Relaxing is nothing to be ashamed of, as far as I know.**

You think you can, but you don't. I could stop if I wanted to. Yah right, but you don't want to stop because they are tasty and you are bored or "busy." You keep going until you feel content.

We all have been carried away at times checking one more email, the weather report, the stock market, and how you can lose five pounds today with the ten top tips given in an attachment. Forget the fact you probably gained two pounds that day sitting at your computer instead of moving around physically. That's why I get up and go to the refrigerator so often when I'm working on the computer. It is for the exercise. The lifting of items to my mouth is a form of weight lifting which helps me to have strong and thin wrists. I also make up stuff to justify my guilt.

In order to get things done you must guard yourself against time wasters like email where you can spend hours just being amused and confused. Deal with the urgent emails and move on.

The telephone can also be a time waster, so you may need to set boundaries at work as to how much time you can afford when you first start a conversation. For example, say to your caller, "I have about five minutes right now before I need to start preparing for an important meeting that will start in an hour. Will that be enough time, or should we reschedule our talk for another time?" Personal calls should be limited to your break times except, of course, for emergencies. Emergencies must be limited to urgent needs of your family. I'd also like to add that not sharing a toy or spilling the cereal does not constitute a true emergency. You need to establish emergency guidelines.

So what is the alternative to being busy? Not being busy sounds like relaxation to me. Relaxing is nothing to be ashamed of, as far as I know. Have we changed the rules or do our own personal backgrounds, culture, or age group stop us from relaxing? We work all our lives so we can retire and have more time to relax. We should really look forward to leisure, which positions relaxing as a form of rejuvenation or "time out" for yourself, in a good way. When we hear that a child is having a "time out," we often ask what he or she did wrong to deserve it. We, as adults, should probably be looking for more "time outs" or "time offs" to get away from it all and recharge our batteries. We have done a lot of things right and deserve to take a break!

Do we think more highly of hard working people who take little time out for themselves, or do we admire those who take a lot of vacations, seem to have a lot of free time, and live quite well according to our standard of thinking? I sometimes secretly wonder if this latter bunch works for the mafia, had very wealthy relatives who died, deals in drugs, or has just won the Power Ball? My initial thinking is usually more of a question as to how they are able to live and support their lifestyles.

I'm also curious about how so many people seem to have so many material things and continue to buy even when they seem to have more than enough? I have heard this behavior called "retail therapy." This is a real addiction. Credit card debt is, sadly, the reason we are seeing people "owning" what they really can't afford and often don't really need – but have it – because it is so easy to get. Do you really need a Global Positioning System in your car? Some people do for some very good reasons, but most of us need to ask one another instead, "Have you ever heard of a map or stopping to ask for directions?" Men aren't well known for the latter. I heard that that is the reason why Moses was in the desert for 40 years.

Those raised in the depression era did not use credit cards. They worked very hard for very little. Working was a constant activity in those days because people had to work to survive. Money usually provided only the things families needed to live a basic life style. I remember a lady in a long term care facility telling me that the reason she kept food in her bedside stand was because, when she would wake up during the night as a little girl, she would be hungry and the family had no food. She was now protecting herself from the gnawing feeling she had in her stomach many years ago which she still vividly remembered to that day. Having food nearby gave her a sense of security that she would never have to go hungry again.

Back in "my day," as we have heard our parents say, we used to eat ketchup sandwiches. George Burns said he used to take the free ketchup packets at the restaurants and put them in hot water to make soup when he was a boy. I remember as a newly married couple that it took three months for us to save up enough to get a $25 light fixture for our dining room. We were both still students working part time with the old fashioned notion that you didn't buy anything if you didn't have the money. We didn't know how to write a check until after we were married. No, the bank wasn't in a covered wagon and the women didn't wear bonnets. Bloomers, yes, bonnets, no.

Is Busy Better?

Times have changed a lot over the last few generations. My cracker jack research comes through again! Are you learning a lot, or what, by reading this book? Our children have not had to do without very much here in America. We are living in an age where there seems to be a lot of frustration, even anger, when people can't have what they want when they want it. Some people get very motivated by those feelings when they believe they need something. They will do whatever it takes to achieve the goals they have set for themselves, legal or illegal. The higher road of honesty has the best scenery.

We were both still students working part time with the old fashioned notion that you didn't buy anything if you didn't have the money.

There are the achievers who find a way or make a way as they try new approaches to make a living while, hopefully, having a life. I heard a new ending for a popular saying that I think you will appreciate: "All things come to those who wait ... but what they get is what is left over from those who hustle."

Many people are not willing to put in the time or energy it takes to do a really good job. They are satisfied with much less than they could have had if they would be willing to put in more effort. We are all different which makes for a very interesting world. As a motivational speaker I am from the school of thought that says, "Why settle for anything less than your best?" Enthusiasm plus effort is unstoppable. The quality of your life is a brain game where, by seeing yourself successful, you are motivated into achieving your goal.

People are discouraged by how much effort it takes to achieve what they would like, so they try to find an easier way, or perhaps they don't even try. They think somehow they will get by or their parents will take care of them forever because, in their eyes, that's what they are supposed to do. That's their job.

We can really hurt our children by not allowing them the opportunity to figure things out for themselves! This goes back to the story of the caterpillar in a cocoon which turned into a butterfly. Someone watching this event cut the cocoon open to assist the butterfly. Instead of taking flight, the butterfly died because it didn't gain the strength it needed by pushing its way out of the cocoon on its own. We need to let our children learn some hard lessons so they will learn to make better choices. Warren Buffet, a well-known multi-millionaire, told reporters that he was going to give a lot of his wealth away because he wants to leave his children "enough so they can do anything, but not so much that they can do nothing."

The motto of my high school graduating class was, "If the elevator isn't running ... take the stairs." That slogan makes a lot more sense to me now than it did then. I learned there were more elevators in my life when I lived at home, and during nurses' training, there were stairs everywhere. There were times some of us threw our text books against the wall saying this is more work than we can possibly do, both physically as we staffed the hospital and mentally as we studied constantly! It seemed impossible! That's when I learned how to take one step at a time and live one moment at a time. I survived by the grace of God! Without the struggle, the accomplishment of becoming a registered nurse would not have meant as much.

> **We can really hurt our children by not allowing them the opportunity to figure things out!**

Is Busy Better?

At our capping ceremony after the first year, we lowered our heads in humility and exhaustion to receive our nursing caps, showing the world that we had made it through that first year. We wore our caps proudly, knowing how much we worked to achieve this symbol of our accomplishments. Caps are now as outdated as cinch belts, hula-hoops, and crinolines worn under poodle skirts. I, however, still think they reflect a reverence for the pride we all had and hopefully still do for the profession

> **It is not a duty but an honor to serve others.**

of nursing. It is not a duty but an honor to serve others. Anything with a worthwhile outcome takes hard work to achieve. No one can give us what we need to be great. We earn the right to be excellent in an area where we have expertise.

The following old adage remains true: "You can give a person a fish so he will eat for a day, or you can teach a person how to fish so he can eat for a lifetime." Which fish dinner would you enjoy more? When you believe in yourself and you achieve whatever it was that you were trying for, there is a great personal satisfaction which can act as a catalyst to future successes.

The lifestyle we do choose usually dictates how busy we need to be in order to keep up with our lifestyle goals. Ask yourself how much is worth what? Are name brands worth the price we pay, or is it better for us to wear what we can really afford and buy a slightly dented appliance or a good used car with low miles once in a while?

There are, however, some very legitimate reasons to be busy in our lives as we provide for ourselves and our families. When we are at work we need to use our talents to provide our employer with quality outcomes from the work we perform which meet or exceed his or her expectations. We need to eliminate the clutter in our lives, concentrate on the task at hand, and focus our energies on achieving the most positive outcome possible. Dr. Laura Pawlik, a bio-chemist, said that the amount of clutter in our lives indicates the health of our brain. O.K., finish the chapter and THEN go clean your desk off or clean that junk drawer out that we all seem to have in common.

We *need* to be busy to at least some degree depending on what season of life we are in. It will, hopefully, be a "good busy" where ideas flow and actions follow. How exhilarating to be "in the game" of making a living while doing what you love doing, knowing that your efforts are making a difference.

> **It's important to remember that experience IS the intelligent use of mistakes.**

Having a positive attitude, being upbeat and a team player never hurt our evaluations either. Enjoying what you do for work is such a plus! You often read about how important it is to find an exercise that is fun because you are more apt to do it regularly.

The same goes for a job. Find something that you really enjoy doing that contributes to something larger than yourself. You will then experience satisfaction in a job well done by someone who cared about what they did. That would be you. How rewarding life can be even when you work full time! Life can be rewarding in a number of ways that we are exploring throughout this book.

Zak Brown, founder and CEO of Just Marketing, Inc., said "Work smart, not hard. You have to be productive and intelligent with your time." That makes a lot of sense, but few, if any of us, will do things the best way first. Good and better need to be experienced before we arrive at best, which means we will make mistakes along the way. It's important to remember that experience IS the intelligent use of mistakes. Tom Peters said, "If you haven't failed lately, you haven't tried much!" It is now time to "Fail Forward," as General Schwartzkopf once said.

The impact of the outcome is determined not only by what you do but by the way you do it, which shows your character as well as your work style. As a nurse I strongly believe the way you administer a medication is often as important as the medication itself. A smile and some polite conversation which relaxes the patient before you do a procedure or give a medication is very helpful for all concerned. The patient's entire system can become more relaxed, facilitating a better delivery of the medication into the body by whatever means.

The emotional climate you set can really make a difference in how things turn out. If you are late and feel rushed, your body will tell everyone who sees you. On the other hand, if you appear calm, collected, and in control, others will gain an immediate confidence in whatever it is you are involved with.

> The impact of the outcome is determined not only by what you do but by the way you do it.

This is true in every line of work. Think of a sales environment. Wouldn't you be much more apt to buy something from people who are relaxed enough to genuinely care about you and your needs? This is probably a perfect time for me to tell you that I care about you, and that you are one of my new best friends. You "need" to read on, and I want you to know that I care whether you do. This book has timeless tips from my lips, which have spilled onto these typed pages in cascades of caring comments meant for you to read.

Remember that we are not at work just to put in our time and get through the day. It is important to contribute more than you cost. We must take charge of our time and use it to produce the greatest value for our employers as well as the customers we serve. We need to give our employers their full dollar value to the best of our ability during working hours.

My younger son called excitedly a short time ago to tell me he had developed some new ways to exceed the expectations of his new boss. He is one of the younger employees and has only worked a few months in a large, leading company known for excellence. He laughed with the joy he felt as he continued to think of innovative ideas to increase sales. He has already proven that what he is doing is working, but he wants to challenge himself to an even greater goal. He is enjoying the results but knows there is a price in time and energy spent.

Lack of sleep is one of the biggest health concerns in a 'too busy' life.

When you look busy at work you are not as apt to be interrupted unnecessarily. Believe it or not, being busy and productive gives us energy. It feels great when we fill a need and accomplish our goals! Hopefully, we have a number of years to embrace and enjoy this kind of energy which, when put into action, delivers the expected results. However, it is excess, like working over fifty hours a week, traveling constantly and having lots of responsibility, that can cause health problems which can be both physical and mental. Pain is one way that our body talks to us when we have been abusing it with too much stress, not enough sleep and an unhealthy diet with little exercise.

Are you at your best when you are stressed? Sometimes the adrenaline we get from stress gives us a competitive edge for a moment but that acuity lessens as we become chronically fatigued from being stressed for long periods. We are so much more effective when we are well rested and in charge of our health instead of leaving our feelings and emotions dictate our actions. I feel like a bowl of ice cream right now but my brain caused me to look down, think, and go on typing, hoping to burn off some of the fat on my fingers.

Out of all the things we do to our bodies, lack of sleep is one of the biggest health concerns in a "too busy" life. When we don't get enough sleep, our bodies lose their natural rhythm to refresh and renew themselves. You may be very surprised at how complex your sleep system really is.

* * *

I am at a season in life, now, where I truly celebrate the successes of others without feeling I am a loser and don't measure up because someone is busier than I am doing things that make more money than I do. I am more concerned when difficult things happen to others, no matter who they are or how affluent they are. I have learned to be a people-builder, especially after experiencing the impact others had on my life by caring enough to take time to encourage and be there for me in my times of need.

> **Where you spend your time and money shows what you value.**

What is really nice is having the time to build others up, showing them that I care by spending time with them. Look in your own day planner/calendar, as well as in your check book, to see what you care about. Where you spend your time and money shows what you value. Caring for and about others seems to be less common in our busy society where taking care of Number One has often been the norm. "I don't have time to think of others" may be a mantra for some. These same people are often the ones who lack joy and meaning in their lives. Many people have a number of acquaintances but few, if any, real friends. To have a friend, you need to BE one, and that takes time and energy. It is, however, one of the investments in our lives that has eternal significance. The only thing you can take to heaven is other people who share a relationship with God.

The Golden Rule is: "Do unto others as you would have them do unto you." The Platinum Rule by Tony Alexander is, "Do unto others as they want done unto them." That means to give people service in the way they want to receive it. One size doesn't fit all. Give people choices and they will respond more readily with greater enthusiasm.

> **The only thing you can take to heaven is other people who share a relationship with God.**

Here's a thought: "Education without enthusiasm is boredom. Enthusiasm without knowledge is energized incompetence!" The message here is to know what you are going to say and be enthusiastic when you share it with others if you want them to remember what you said. A knowledgeable employee who is also enthusiastic is continually being sought after by employers because these employees know what to say and are enjoyable to be around. Another way to be sought after, not only as an employee but as a friend, is to be a good listener.

According to Career Builder author Lisa Radke, a racing mind is to blame for not properly hearing others when they speak. It is important to stay in the moment when listening to others. Don't prepare your reply while the other person is still speaking. We sometimes are so busy mentally planning a rebuttal that we may miss the other person's true message as well as the meaning behind the message.

Our minds drift because we think at a speed which is much faster than when others talk. When listening at a high speed, our minds fade in and out. To prevent this and stay engaged, we must focus on the other person's meaning as well as the motivation behind it. Demonstrate your interest by asking them to tell you more about the subject. You'll find that, when you listen more than you talk, people generally comment on what a great conversationalist you are. Listening is an art. It should be nurtured and practiced just like we would if we were preparing for a presentation. Look people in the eye when they are speaking and don't allow anything to distract you, if at all possible. Great listeners often take notes, nod to encourage the person speaking and ask good questions.

Here's a good question: "Have you noticed that life is not fair or predictable?" I overheard someone say, "If life didn't suck, we would all fall off." Now that is pretty candid! A lady and I were walking out of a building together on a beautiful day a couple of days after Hurricane Katrina hit New Orleans. She spread her arms open, looked up into the beautiful sky and said, "We are so rich!" She and I took that moment to stop and share an experience of genuine gratitude as we recognized the beauty around us. We would have missed that beautiful moment if we had been too preoccupied with ourselves or too caught up in the hurry of life.

> Grab moments when things are beautiful around you, and dwell in them for a moment of celebration.

I try to be constantly aware of how many people there are in the world who are in places where they cannot say the sky is beautiful. There may be disastrous weather conditions, car bombs blackening the sky, or fires out of control. Grab moments when things are beautiful around you, and dwell on them for a moment of celebration.

I Only Have a Minute ... So Let's Make It Matter!

Stopping to share something we feel passionate about in an emotional moment binds people together, especially in uncertain times. May we learn to never take our good moments for granted! Bathe yourself in the beauty of quiet contentment as you learn about the empowerment that a relaxed countenance can provide. People are attracted to you when you appear relaxed, available, and yet passionate about life. Do remember that everyone is not going to like, much less love, you no matter how much good you do. Ask Jesus. We simply have to live with this in mind, and move on to someone with better taste.

One huge benefit I have noticed when I am relaxed and not hurried is that I get more creative. My mind gets playful when it is recharged. My body joins in with some silly behavior like when I purchased a hat at Busch Gardens that was in the shape of a hot dog. Ever walk around a public place with a hot dog hat on your head, but with a serious look on your face that says, "This is normal for me"? What is normal? Someone once told me that normal is a setting on your clothes dryer. I buy that. Normal is all "relative" in my world because they know me there. My "relatives" just roll their eyes when I act weird. Weird is wonderful. It is a form of release from reality.

When I am relaxed I am more apt to exaggerate my think-ing. I take time to look at where I am, who I am with, and what we are doing, along with what is silly about the whole situation. What would make this moment in time even more fun? Fun is more important to me than remaining busy, although having fun keeps me busy in my mind since, at times, there is not a lot going on in there. When that happens, there is more room to play.

A neighbor was having a garage sale so I walked over and found a monkey on one of the tables that hangs around your neck with little arms and with hands that stick to one another with Velcro. I liked it right off, so I put its little arms around my neck and walked around in the sale starting conversations with the customers. I told them the monkey liked what they were looking at, and the monkey said they should buy it. One customer said that was the most fun garage sale she had ever been to ... and all because of a silly monkey and a strange neighbor. Being playful is actually contagious. Before long being silly sets in, and infectious laughter starts to spread.

Now, back to my original question: "Is being busy really better?" My answer is, "Not always," or "Sometimes." So much for the expert opinion you were expecting! We have determined that "good busy" is necessary and can make us very productive so we can earn what we need to live and then some. How I spend the precious commodity of my time left here on earth is more about what and who I value than about what I have materially. I truly believe happiness is inside our hearts and not in what we wear, drive or possess. It all goes back to the old question of what do we NEED versus what do we WANT. My needs have become more simple as I realize how truly blessed I am compared to so many in the world who don't even have their basic needs met. Consider the following:

If you woke up this morning with more health than illness, you are more blessed than the million who won't survive the week.

If you have never experienced the danger of battle, the loneliness of imprisonment, the agony of torture or the pangs of starvation, you are ahead of 20 million people around the world.

If you attend a church meeting without fear of harassment, arrest, torture, or death, you are more blessed than almost three billion people in the world.

If you have food in your refrigerator, clothes on your back, a roof over your head and a place to sleep, you are richer than 75 percent of this world.

I Only Have a Minute ... So Let's Make It Matter!

If you have money in the bank, in your wallet, and spare change in a dish someplace, you are among the top 8 percent of the world's wealthy.

If your parents are still married and alive, you are very rare, especially in the United States.

If you hold up your head with a smile on your face and are truly thankful, you are blessed because the majority can, but most do not.

If you can read this message, you are more blessed than over two billion people in the world who cannot read anything at all.

We are so blessed in so many ways that we may never even realize. Awareness is the beginning of wisdom.

Those are statistics and thoughts sent from one of my favorite writers, ANON, who writes actively on the internet. They are statistics that make us aware that we do have more than "enough," even if we don't have cable television. There are things called books that are a great way to learn, laugh, and keep you interested in life without using an electric plug. They also help you relax without being over stimulated with some type of noise going on around you.

I have decided to be as busy as I need to be to meet the needs of my family, but I no longer feel that I have to have constant activity in my life in order to feel useful and worthwhile. There is a difference between being driven and being realistically involved in activities that generate an income, to provide for the needs of your family.

Former first lady, Barbara Bush, had some wonderful things to say about how to get the "busy-ness" out of our lives. Her comments have to do with being more patient. She writes: *"Impatience stems almost solely from our exaggerated notions of what is due us. If we could but lower our estimation of the importance of our time, our plans and our feelings, we would find ourselves almost automatically more patient. Patience is the ability to bear affliction, delay, or an interruption with calmness, perseverance and confidence in the goodness of God. (Colossians 1:11-12). It is inward peace as well as outward control. God has a good reason for every delay he allows to come our way."*

Happiness is inside your heart and not in what you wear, drive, or possess. Time is finite. You cannot save time, make up time or add minutes to your day. There is only so much. Interesting, however, how time does seem to stand still if you go stand in a line somewhere. The time is the same, but it just seems longer when you are waiting.

Tic, tock, tic tock ... 86,400 seconds
each day is all we've got.
Is being busy going to affect
the hands upon the clock?

"No," said the hands. "I do not care
that you are rushing all about.
"My job is to keep going and be accurate
before my battery runs out."

We are not perfect; I cannot do all I would like
or all I said.
My eyes are starting to close ... it is time for me
to finally go to bed.

Busy is not better, I have learned from life
and all that I have read.
You won't believe me until one day
you finally wake up and it's too late ... you're dead.

- Kathy Brown

Chapter Five
The Art of Positive Aging

Life is this incredible journey which takes us through seasons in which we grow physically and mentally while learning some meaningful lessons along the way. The seasons change with different activities and influences that affect us as babies, children, adolescents, then on to adulthood, ranging from being young adults to middle age to senior citizens. Aging is quite popular ... everyone is doing it! We do the best we can for as long as we can. The length of our journey is affected by our choices, which determine our destiny. Some times we don't have a choice, but that is part of our human condition.

I think of aging as an art because you can craft your own tomorrows by how you think and by what you do with your today. Some days I feel like a flawed canvas, but I know we were fashioned by the Master whose perfect plan makes no mistakes – just opportunities to rely and trust in Him even more as He completes each Masterpiece.

One of the arts in positive aging is the art of hospitality. The biblical translation means "a love of strangers." Inviting someone in for coffee, offering to baby-sit, taking a meal to someone who is sick ... all show that we care. And people listen to someone who cares. We are drawn to people who make time for

I Only Have a Minute ... So Let's Make It Matter!

others. They are certainly easier to relate to and seem to listen more intently. Their body language tells a story as they practice their language of love by serving others.

There is another art ... listening. Listening is a critical skill that immediately draws you to someone who has mastered the art. When we truly listen, focusing all of our energy into really hearing what another person is saying, we have shared an important gift. It is the gift of our time along with our caring. Expensive? No. Priceless? Yes. How you make others feel can make or break their day. Isn't that alone worth the investment?

Another very important investment is our health. Our health is our greatest wealth. We need to invest in it daily so we have the energy and physical resources we need for the challenges that our body faces every day on this journey through life. As we age, we are hopefully accumulating financial assets to store up for our golden years, but even more importantly, we need to be accumulating habits that will build our bodies into very nice places in which to live. Wouldn't you rather live in a comfortable home than under a bridge? The bridge may seem like a "cool" thing to try, but your brain will usually kick in after a short time with a reality check that should be cashed immediately for best results. Choices that may be fun to try may become habits that can hurt and make you cry and even make you die. You will then understand the importance of making good choices in your health habits – if you are not already dead.

> How you make others feel can make or break their day. Isn't that alone worth the investment?

Our bodies should be a healthy place to live if we plan to stay around. An unhealthy body can be a "real pain" to live in. Why live in a shack when you can occupy a castle? I know that my "home body" has added a larger front porch with a deck in the back. I have been trying to downsize the last few years, which is a constant struggle as the structure keeps settling. If I would stop buying the wrong building materials – like snack food and desserts "in case the kids come" – I would have a more fuel efficient place to hang out. Unfortunately, I am hanging out more and enjoying it less. I hope to tear down the additions, one calorie at a time. I was on a stationary bicycle at the health

> ## Nothing tastes as good as being fit feels.

club peddling as fast as I could for a whole five minutes. When I saw that I had burned up only 26 calories in that mini marathon, I said right out loud, "That's only an Altoid!" I just burnt off enough calories to enjoy one whole Altoid, which, for those of you who don't know, is a breath mint.

When I am under attack with deadlines and expectations, I have, in the past, volleyed back ... with a snack. I found a great saying that I have taped to my desk to encourage me when I get a "snack attack." It says "nothing tastes as good as being fit feels!" Underneath this wonderful statement, I wrote in red ink, "Walk it off, Snack Fairy!" This may seem blunt, but I have found that you have to get tough with your cellulite. Otherwise it multiplies itself in weak moments when there is no one around to hug or talk to. That is when wrapping yourself around a big bowl of buttered pop corn makes perfect sense. And then, before you can blink your eye, there is a can of root beer in the other hand – the one you are not using to push the pop corn into your mouth. This gives you a momentary "feel good" feeling which, unfortunately, does not last. The pop corn and pop, however, rush right to your butt.

"You are as good as you feel" is an old saying with some true merit. It is hard to be at the top of your game when your body is in the dugout of despair, either mentally or physically, which can cause us to crave food ... or many other things too numerous to mention. Too much of anything can be harmful. We can, however, take our thoughts captive and think ourselves into actually feeling better physically than we actually are.

Unfortunately, we oftentimes don't give our health much thought until something goes wrong. Pain is a signal that tells us something is wrong. When we're in pain, we probably need a "tune up," which should include a mental "tune in" to our lifestyle habits. What are we doing to ourselves that may contribute to the pain we are now feeling?

> **Positive thinking often results in positive behavior changes.**

T.S. Eliot observed, "People are only influenced in the direction in which they want to go, and influence consists largely in making them conscious of their wishes to proceed in that direction." In other words we are going to do what we want anyway, but you may do something sooner if it's brought to your attention. Hello ... anyone home to hear this?

Positive thinking often results in positive behavior changes. Since change is the engine of growth, the NEW changed thinking will hopefully encourage us to self assess, think the best, and get more rest. A rested body is the most underrated source of health and vitality available, according to "The Complete Idiot's Guide To Getting a Good Night's Sleep," by Martin Moore Ede, M.D., Ph.D., who sounds like someone we should listen to when we are trying our best NOT to look like an idiot. That is one of my long range goals.

Falling asleep in front of others is a little tacky so take note of your answers to the following questions:

• Am I getting enough sleep to meet my body's requirements which are unique to me? According to the National Sleep

Foundation, more than 30 percent of American drivers admit to falling asleep while driving. An estimated 100,000 accidents and 1,500 fatalities each year are attributed to falling asleep at the wheel. The direct cost of human fatigue on the nation is estimated at 70 billion dollars.

- Are you tense and driven in your activities throughout the day, i.e., "Stressed for Success"? A tense muscle is a slow muscle. Our productivity lessens when we are on overload. We need to learn how to relax as much as we need to work in order to be our balanced best. Stress occurs when the amount of pressure is greater than the amount of resources stock-piled by our body in an effort to compensate.

- Are you drinking enough water every day? Did you know that, according to Drs. Ronald Klatz and Robert Goldman, drinking too little water speeds up aging? As we get older, the need for water increases. Drink at least eight glasses a day, but 10 to 12 glasses of water is best. Water also lowers your body temperature which can help burn fat calories. If you meet me and I am carrying a canteen, you will now understand

> **A rested body is the most underrated source of health and vitality available.**

that it is part of my "be fit, not fat" campaign because drinking water has been proven to help you lose weight.

I know those little fat calorie people personally. I KNOW where to find them because they are not hiding like they used to. They like to hang out together because they are friends and have bonded with one another. Well, I want to lose those friends and make NEW friends with Mr. Fiber and Mrs. Protein. They sound more solid and well connected.

I Only Have a Minute ... So Let's Make It Matter!

Actually, I did get help from a fitness trainer. Fitness trainers are the ones who tell you the right way to exercise, then you do it your way ... and they have a "fit." Simply showing up regularly is the hardest part for me. It helps if I weigh the difference of what I will get done at my job against how much better I will feel and how much more effective I will be if I get up and exercise. Better choices are a thought a way. I will start today. Every day is a new beginning, so don't get discouraged — get moving!

Learning to like exercise starts in your mind. Motion follows your emotions. Think of some exercise that you enjoy doing. Napping is NOT an official exercise, even though your eyelids may open and close a few times. That does not count. Note: Consciousness is that annoying time between naps when you can and should exercise.

Dancing is one of my favorite ways to exercise. It is a wonderful series of motions set to rhythm. Vibrational healing triggers brain cells that burn fat. Let's have a bonfire! Passion is a vital mindset to everyone who wants to age well. Use it or lose it. Aspire to perspire, and be inspired before you expire. It is truly up to each of us to start our own fire to light the way to learn more so we can continue to improve or maintain our health as we age.

> **Motion follows your emotions.**

We have no one but ourselves to blame for those extra pounds. I know because I've tried. My grandmother was overweight so I figured that it must be in my genes. No, the extra fat is in my "jeans" ... the ones with the stretchy waist band. My friend said she used to go skinny dipping but now she goes "chunky dunking." It helps to share our pain and laugh about it while we are in the process of "doing" something about it. My fun loving neighbor said she wants to put one of those "wide load" signs on her backside when she goes for a walk on the street. You gotta love her! (And I do!)

I make jokes about my weight because it helps me cope, but I am seriously wanting to lose at least a thigh. My husband is a man with a slight build, so I feel like his "chunky chick." In jest, I told him that if he "porked up" a little, I wouldn't look so big. He is very self disciplined and works out about five times a week. I did get a personal trainer a couple of months ago ... to visit with. Actually, I now have a plan as well as a number of exercises to do each time I show up. No show – no fat go.

> **Passion is a vital mindset to everyone who wants to age well.**

When I was at our local health club recently, I saw a petite young woman wearing these really cute shorts that read "Augsburg College" on the back of them. I was feeling a little chunky that day, so when I came home I told my husband about the cute young lady in the adorable shorts hoping he would say something to make me feel better. Looking for a little affirmation, I said, "My shorts could read University of California." My husband looked at me soberly and added, "At Berkeley." We both paused for a moment and then started to laugh heartily. The ability to laugh at yourself is a real stress buster! Ken really deserved a "time out" for that one, but I set myself up for it so I humbly let it go with a huge smile which may have burnt up about one calorie.

Lately, I have been working out at CURVES, as well, which is helping me get even better results and enjoy the process of exercising more as I socialize my way into a smaller size with ladies of all sizes. Socializing is a very positive piece in the process of positive aging. We laugh and learn, share and care, listen and glisten with small drops of perspiration as we exercise our way to wellness while making new friends.

The good news is that it's never too late to reap the benefits of exercising. In fact, the older you are, the more immediate benefit you get from exercise. Exercise is the solution for almost every health problem, but it especially makes sense in dealing with the stressors that are common during each season of our lives. That's because our bodies respond to stress by boosting energy into the muscles, so using those muscles during exercise is an obvious outlet for releasing stress.

> It is not
> how old you are,
> but how you are old.

Tara Parker-Pope's research on aging shows that how well we age is tied to our two most basic personality traits: the social relationships we have and our ability to cope with stress. Robert Sapolsky, a Stanford University neuroendocrinologist, said aging is about a body that doesn't deal well with stress anymore. One third of aging is hereditary and the rest is acquired, so we truly are responsible for how well we age. I personally believe that it is not how old you are, but HOW you are old. How old you really feel involves your perception of yourself as well as your self confidence. When we have a high level of self confidence, it creates a positive impact on our health.

Successful agers are not loners who keep to themselves. People who age the best tend to be close to their extended family, have a strong network of friends, and enjoy many social relationships. Having friends and family in your life increases the likelihood that you will get out more and keep moving. This does not mean in a truck with your furniture, either.

Personality traits such as optimism, adaptability, and a willingness to try new things are linked to better aging. Hire the happy at any age. They are more fun to work with! Be with happy people and you will be happier. Fun is definitely contagious without any negative side effects.

An important key in aging positively is to continually learn new things so our brains stay stimulated. Basically, we don't know what we don't know. We know we're supposed to eat fresh fruit and whole grain foods the way nature intended, spend lots of time being active, get plenty of sleep, be around people we love, and not get overly stressed. We can do that for longer periods if we allow extra time to do things and to get to places. You will also have greater peace of mind if you have backups like an extra car key in your wallet, an extra house key buried in a potted plant, extra stamps, and some extra cash on hand.

> Personality traits such as optimism, adaptability, and a willingness to try new things are linked to better aging.

Another good idea is to have your car filled up with gas just in case you need to make a quick trip for something and don't have time to spare to go to your favorite gas station. Your favorite gas station, if you are like most of us, is the one with the cheapest gas. My economical 84-year-old mother drives around to find the best price for gas. She has taught me to clip coupons, save Betty Crocker box labels for free stuff, and we dare not forget those Gold Bond Stamps of yesteryear where we could save up for some exciting items in a catalog. I was trained by a seasoned pro on how to get the best value for my dollar which made "sense" to me then, and still does to this day. My husband has opened our newspaper more than once only to find holes in it. He just keeps reading, acknowledging the fact that he married a "clip-towomaniac." Which is the female version of a cleptomaniac who clips.

I Only Have a Minute ... So Let's Make It Matter!

My daughter called me shortly after she was married exclaiming, "Mom, I'm becoming like you!" I was silent for just a moment, then asked somewhat guardedly, "What have you done, dear one?" She confessed that she had clipped coupons before she went grocery shopping and actually used almost every one of them. She then remarked candidly, "I used to hate that when I went shopping with you. I was embarrassed back then, but you know what?" (I couldn't wait to hear.) "I saved $3.25, and John seemed pleased." We both began giggling, realizing that some of the things we pass on are from the wisdom of our elders who lived their values in front of us. We called it cheap then, and we call it economical now.

Being a good steward of our resources still feels good since whatever we have, in my thinking, is all on loan to us from God anyway. What we do with it is our gift back to Him. I try to do what has the most value with my time as well as my money these days. Clipping coupons has almost dropped off the charts now, although I still get spurts of frugality like when I see a Dairy Queen ad for a buy one blizzard and get one free.

> Experiences are the intelligent use of mistakes.

You NEED to buy one at this point to teach your children and grandchildren the importance of saving money. It's your job. Besides, then you have a good reason to go back to the health club or CURVES to socialize again, which is a necessary part of positive aging. A brisk walk with a neighbor can do wonders as well. Or you could do sit ups, but let's get real. My stomach gets mad when I keep smashing it like a compactor. The only result I've seen is a firmer folded droop of tummy flab.

* * *

If you want to do well at your job, remember the impor-tance of a positive attitude which needs to adapt constantly in this ever changing world. We need to learn to let go of things that are no longer relevant and embrace the new, more challenging ways because they are the future. We are not going to "get it" at first and will make errors. Remember that, according to Tom Peters, author of "In Search Of Excellence," we are to fail forward and learn how to stop our failures faster. Part of the art of positive aging is to be aware of our need to forgive others, hoping and trusting that they will also forgive us in return.

Let us not forget, or better yet, choose to believe, that most people are doing the best they can. Remember that experiences are the intelligent use of mistakes, so don't be too hard on yourself or others. *Romans 12:10: "Be kindly affectionate to one another with brotherly love, in honor giving preference to one another."* Can you imagine a whole world that actually practiced those principles? Right now it seems it is "every man for himself" doing things "their" way all over the world.

> Living healthy lives demands a higher level of skill and health awareness.

It may help to remind ourselves daily that we are not the general manager of the universe. Just controlling ourselves can be a full time job. Real life doesn't make this easy with our busy lives, sedentary pastimes, the volume of unhealthy foods we eat, the pressures of a consumer society, and the peddling of fast answers to our every concern.

So what about that stuff we don't know we don't know? Living healthy lives demands a higher level of skill and health awareness. There are a gazillion (well almost) articles in papers, magazines, and on-line that you can read for every health care issue. If you want to know about something, you can find out more readily now than ever before. Just saying, "I don't know," is really a way of saying, "I just don't care." We need to take charge of our health and care enough to find answers to our questions and solutions to our concerns.

Aging positively is also based on our perceptions. Psychologist, Kathleen Papatola says many of our reactions to aging are determined by how we see what goes on around us. The adage that time crawls by for the young while flying by for the old is based on perception. One year to a 10-year-old is ten percent of his or her life. One year to a fifty year old is only 2 percent. Ten percent of something is a much bigger proportion than two percent of the same thing, when you do the math. I took my shoes off, so trust me.

I feel math impaired at times, but that is why God made calculators. He didn't want our brain to blow up when it got filled up with figures. My figure is all ready filled up. It almost blew up while we were on vacation. Actually, there were small explosions of calories detonated by ice cream. I do not fear loosing weight. In fact I look forward to seeing less of me. Fear can be a real problem, however, especially as we age.

Fear of losses, rather than the anticipation of gains, colors our perception of aging in a number of ways. Anticipating loss keeps us from moving ahead. All too often, aging is a process of looking backward instead of forward. It reminds us of lives past instead of experiences yet to be lived. Looking back undermines the potential and sabotages our confidence. Reflecting on positive memories, however, can bring comfort when we reflect on the good times we shared with our family and friends. Looking ahead provides a key to new opportunities and challenges. It's a way to reconcile parts of our past and move ahead to a future with more of our own creative design. Aging is inevitable, but how we choose to age is a product of perception. Perception is the one thing we can control. Don't you just love that part?

The Art of Positive Aging

In my quest for knowledge, which is also required to keep my nursing license current, I completed a class on aging from the Institute for Natural Resources where I learned twelve quick tips to help us live longer and function well. These are things you will recognize as good health habits unless you have been trapped in a capsule and have not had any contact with learning. They are worth reviewing along with a bit of my own insight to enhance the value of your reading experience. Enhancing is fancy, and it adds a little fun as well!

Good Health Habits	Kathy's Insights
1. Don't smoke (or stop smoking)	Do everyone a favor
2. Drink less alcohol	You will think more clearly
3. Keep weight steady	Not gaining is a victory
4. Eat fewer calories	Use smaller bowls and dishes
5. Eat fruits and vegetables	Add fun condiments to perk them up
6. Take your vitamins	Can't eat enough food to get what you need
7. Exercise regularly	Not just when "you have the time"
8. Sleep well	Wind down before bedtime
9. Challenge your mind	Do things that make you think
10. Have a positive attitude	Being negative can make you sick
11. Don't let stress build up	Repeat: "I'm too blessed to be stressed"
12. Stay friendly and social	Smile. Make someone else feel special

I Only Have a Minute ... So Let's Make It Matter!

Our lifestyle has a direct influence on how long we live. Not only did we get our genes from our parents, but we also inherited their habits, to some degree, such as how we live and what we eat and how we handle stress. Life style habits can strongly influence how our genes function. You can choose to change to a healthier lifestyle.

Did you know that people in Asian countries rank highest in longevity? They eat more natural foods but are not as productive business-wise because they mostly enjoy rural living. The tug between work and family is one of the highest sources of stress and anxiety for us. Our work and home life need to be in harmony in order to have a life that is truly both rich and rewarding. Our work habits can jeopardize not only our happiness but also the overall happiness of our immediate family.

I remember working nursing shifts from 3 p.m. to 11 p.m. with three children at home who were involved in a variety of activities that required transportation other than their feet. My husband did take them, but I missed being in the stands cheering them on. I would call home sometimes to hear everyone laughing about something that I was missing out on.

It seems a little strange to me that people who seem "driven" by their work often feel ashamed for wanting balanced lives. This is especially true for those of us in the health care field where being short staffed is almost a given, along with the sense that we are the ones who need to take care of the world. We do need to be reminded that our work is only one piece of our lives, and hopefully not "THE most important."

> The tug between work and family is one of the highest sources of stress and anxiety for us.

To obtain the balance we crave, we need to establish some boundaries and limitations which are often difficult to enforce. I have become much better at controlling the amount of time I spend working so as not to miss out on quality family time now that our population of grandchildren has exploded. The people I want to influence the most still wear a lot of diapers and need time with "silly Nanna." I have just lately had to give up giving horsie rides which I have thoroughly enjoyed doing for a number of years. My chiropractor warned me that, otherwise, I may soon resemble Don Quixote's horse. We need to listen to those educated opinions, because we may be too close emotionally to a situation to make the best decision. I also work like a horse, which is supposed to be a good thing. Working for myself gives me better breaks, longer lunch hours, and a pretty positive work environment, depending on my mood. The only drawback is that when I call in sick, I know that I am lying. None of us can avoid stress all together because stress is life. It is the degree of stress and the duration of it that dictates how much it really affects our mental and physical health.

> **Our greatest energy comes from our emotions.**

If our world seems out of order, we will have more stress. Each one of us has our own sense of order. Don't touch my desk! There is tranquility in order, so if you keep your life in order, you will be calmer and better able to handle stress. Did you know that the amount of clutter you allow is an indicator of your state of mind? When your surroundings are organized, you are able to focus, which helps memory. People with ADHD have problems going from global thinking to focusing because focusing takes a lot of energy, which they are not always able to give. We need energy to get the things done that matter to us. Less stress means better aging, which results in a longer, less complicated life that we all can enjoy even more.

Our greatest energy comes from our emotions. We remember things we are passionate about because we care about those things. The way we think and feel affects our body. We don't always feel like getting out of bed at the same time everyday. We need a purpose to get out of bed. Volunteering is a wonderful way to add purpose to our lives, especially when we are not working for pay. Life is to cope with and contribute to with the talents we are given. Make a list of things that would be enjoyable to contribute your time and talent to when you do have the time. If your time doesn't matter you won't know what time it is.

* * *

People respond to the energy and ideas of others. We need to keep stimulating our mind as well as our body, with ideas and movement. Challenge yourself constantly to stimulate your senses because that is what keeps your brain and body alive. Keep all of your senses working! Memory is the key to survival. If you cannot remember what was said, you don't want to talk. If you don't talk, you don't think, and then you don't move.

> ### Shut off your television and become a more interesting person yourself!

Some movements of others can generate anger. Anger never solves anything. If someone is angry with you on the highway (i.e., road rage), smile at them when they drive by and say very clearly as they stare at you, "I LOVE YOU!" That, believe it or not, has caused people to stare back in disbelief and just drive off. Anger erases years off your life. Don't be around negative people for long because they can bring you down. Be the type of person you like to be around. Shut off your television and become a more interesting person yourself! Read a book a week to stimulate your senses so you will have more to talk about. Your communication skills will help you become memorable.

The Art of Positive Aging

Be memorable to those who matter in your life. Memorable people make memories that people remember long after you have left this world. People respond to energy! When we are listening to boring people we often don't remember what they even say. You don't need to wear a lamp shade to be memorable, but a nice parrot hat with huge green and white eyes placed straight on your head so the tail goes down the back of your neck might work! You are in luck! I just happen to have such a hat that I picked up on our last trip. My husband just rolled his eyes, grinned and said, "It's really you, honey."

Did you know that laughter actually prolongs your life? This book, as you now know, is filled with needed knowledge that you may not even have known that you needed. If you laugh daily, smile a lot, have people who love you in your life, and make fun a daily routine, you will have a greater chance of living longer. Being fit and having fun can be done. Try it. Your life will like it.

> ## I look at the retirement years as a time to turn up the fun meter.

Research shows that people recover from setbacks, either physical or mental, twice as fast if they have someone with them who cares. Relationships are critical to positive aging in every season of our lives. You cannot build a meaningful relationship on a cell phone, i.e., "just touching base, will call again later, love you ... bye." Meaningful relationships are well worth the investment of time and commitment that it takes to make them last.

Friends who are playful and fun to be around double your investment in the fine art of positive aging. When we call the home of our retired friends, they answer, "Emporium of Happiness." I smile every time I call them, anticipating the crazy conversations that are sure to follow after that opening line which sets a playful tone right from the start. I look at the retirement

I Only Have a Minute ... So Let's Make It Matter!

years as a time to turn up the fun meter. The children have set sail and so should we – into the uncharted waters of adventure with less responsibility.

When I am not pressured by deadlines, I get a lot more playful. In fact, I seek out "silly stuff" to do. My precious and patient husband, Ken, was recently working at his desk at home looking way too serious as he poured over some forms. I decided it was time for him to take a break. I walked up behind him wearing a large hat in the shape of a hot dog that I purchased at Busch Gardens and started to sing "I wish I were an Oscar Meyer wiener." He was forced to acknowledge my presence as I circled him and asked if he would like to have a turn wearing the hot dog hat while we sang together. He gave me a tolerant look, asking if I had extra time on my hands. I did see a smirk, however, which, for an engineer may be interpreted as a gut busting laugh. That was enough for me as I laughed and left, knowing in my heart that I had helped him take a much needed break.

You need to know that this man has been conditioned to expect that anything can happen at any given moment when I am around. I do this kind of thing every so often just to keep him on his toes so he stays on the alert for the unknown fun factor.

> **Why not approach retirement as an adventure with endless possibilities to make a positive difference?**

If retirement to you means "doing nothing," it can be the kiss of death, according to Ken Dychtwald, an authority on aging, who says that the transition can be much like an adolescent trying to figure out what to do next. Why not approach retirement as an adventure with endless possibilities to make a positive difference? America's 77 million baby boomers are heading into retirement with more of a sense of its possibilities and challenges than any previous generation. At this writing, the Baby Boomers are turning 60 and they are going to set a new standard as "seasoned citizens."

Sixty to eighty years old is "Prime Time" for awe, wonder, and appreciation. People in this age range are the OWLS, which stands for "older, wiser, livelier souls." There are new opportunities and activities for these "Geri-Actives." They like to say they are not retiring but re-

> To worry is to be stressed about something you may feel little or no control over.

firing. Re-wirement is what 59-year-old Virginia Monaghan of Pennsylvania likes to call this time of life. This is the giving stage where seniors now have time to give back and to make wonderful things happen that they never had the time for before.

Retirement lifts most people into euphoria for about a year and then drops them into a new reality, according to a new study on retirement reality by Harris Interactive for Ameriprise Financial. The study's key finding is that people who started planning early, had a vision of retirement, and stayed active reported the most satisfaction in retirement, according to Craig Brimhall, Vice President of Ameriprise Financial. We need to be attuned to what people are retiring to, rather than what they are retiring from, he says. The study defined four distinct retiree profiles from the next two to fifteen years after retirement: "empowered re-inventors" (19 percent), "carefree contents" (19 percent), "uncertain searchers" (22 percent), and "worried strugglers" (40 percent).

To worry is to be stressed about something you may feel little or no control over. You lose serotonin when you are stressed. It is true, and it has consequences.

I Only Have a Minute ... So Let's Make It Matter!

We can raise our serotonin levels according to Dr. Laura Pawlak, Ph.D., M.S., R.D. with four steps. First, be in a lighted area – either natural or artificial. Second, exercise. Third, get more sleep. A well rested body is a good companion. The fourth way is having friends. Yes! Meaningful friendships boost your serotonin level.

People who boost your level are more than acquaintances. They are people who you know on a deeper level and whom you can trust. Dr. Pawlak told us that if we are saving a seat for a friend who boosts your serotonin level and another person sits down, we must tell that person to get up and move somewhere else because we are saving the seat for a good friend who gives us serotonin. I really enjoyed her humorous insight, especially while she taught about chemical relationships, which can be about as exciting as watching a dog sleep.

> The greatest challenges in life do not come from around us, but from within us.

Making a serious topic exciting can be a challenge, but the greatest challenges in life do not come from around us, but from within us. An important key for healthy aging is to get in touch with contentment and simplicity. This is more challenging to do in America because many people have chosen stress as a lifestyle so they can keep up with their friends and neighbors. We must choose for ourselves the lifestyle that makes the most sense for our lives, family, and circumstances. Sometimes we have no choice for survival except to work a lot. We can, however, choose to stop and re-charge so our batteries don't get run down to the point of having health issues. Our bodies have a way of telling us that we have crossed the line and are not as healthy as we could be. We may ignore these signs, so my advice to you is "watch for signs" that indicate you are not at your finest and need a tune up.

The Art of Positive Aging

I started to have reflux after speaking eight times in five days in a variety of locations that required air travel during Nurses Week one year. My body started to visit with me about the scheduling of my life. I am passionate about celebrating nurses at any time, but Nurses Week is THE special week when health care institutions thank nurses formally for their dedication to serving others. Been there, done that, and I know how good that feels when people appreciate the work you do. The positive energy of encouragement is always appreciated, no matter what you do for a living! I did get help for that condition, which has since resolved itself, at least for now, as I quietly write this book.

Appreciating everyone would make a wonderful life mission which certainly would contribute to everyone aging more positively. My husband and I once were in a card shop. I kept calling him over to read different cards I said I would send to him. He told me, after reading the first couple of cards, "Those are fun. Now when we are done here I want to take you to the flower shop next door and show you the flowers I would have bought you." Ughhh. Lesson learned: Do and give instead of think and say. We need to give our love legs, and do the nice things for one another throughout the year instead of just thinking about people and never doing anything to show them that you do care. I guess that's why the old saying "actions speak louder than words" came into being. Speaking of "action" reminds me of laughter, which simulates "inner jogging" – a very fun action.

> The positive energy of encouragement is always appreciated, no matter what you do!

Laughing at ourselves gives our families and friends permission to jump in with some clever thoughts they might otherwise throw out because they know you will take them with the right spirit, and you will laugh with them. People who really know and love you can say some pretty funny things that would hurt other people's feelings. But you, dear loved one, are fair game.

One year I had put on a few pounds eating comfort foods, for insulation purposes, as winter was fast approaching. When I was bending over to pick up a Christmas gift that year, my older son blurted out with a chuckle in his voice, "What's big and tan, and looks like a mini-van." Everyone fell down laughing. I couldn't help but smile, laughing a little as I looked for a piece of coal to give my smart mouth first born.

There are times for all of us when we don't feel very fun especially when we are overtired. We may get a little snippy or a little snappy perhaps, over small matters. People living years ago, before electricity, went to bed early because it was dark. They slept until it was light. Sounds like an uncomplicated life to me where being overtired was probably not the biggest health concern, unlike today where it has a major impact on our health status. In today's world, by the time you read the paper after work and go through all the junk mail, you could be sporting an "Attitude" because you are just plain tired. When we try to keep going to finish just one more thing instead of going to bed at a decent hour, we are compromising our own health and well being. Why do some of us push ourselves to get just one more thing done? Will the "gitter done" police arrest us for not living up to our own expectations? As we age, we have the luxury of lowering our expectations for what we think must get done on any particular day. We hopefully get a lot better at setting limits.

On the other hand, George Bernard Shaw had a different spin on work which I found to be a real inspiration to those of us who have served or continue to serve others with passion. He said, "I am of the opinion that my life belongs to the whole community, and, as long as I live, it is my privilege to do for the community whatever I can. I want to be thoroughly used up when

I die, for the harder I work the more I live. I rejoice in life for its own sake. Life is no brief candle to me. It is a sort of splendid torch which I've got to hold up for the moment, and I want to make it burn as brightly as possible before passing it on to future generations."

Have you discovered the highest within you yet? I don't think I have because I choose to look forward everyday to making it an even better day for those I have the privilege to be around. May the artist in us make a contribution today to someone else's tomorrow because we passed their way.

Chapter Six

Good Grief

When we love people we set ourselves up for sorrow. The reason for that is because someday we all will be separated one way or another from those we love. For example, we will all die one day as death takes its inevitable toll. English poet Alfred Lord Tennyson must have had this feeling when he penned, "Better to have loved and lost than never to have loved at all." The joy we experience in knowing people well is the trade off for really missing them when they are gone from us, whether by death or divorce.

Divorce can be even more difficult than death because the person you loved no longer loves or wants to be with you. The pain of rejection is incredible! I know that for a fact. My husband of 22 years said he needed to leave and "find" himself after starting a new job working the relief shift with younger people. The details are not necessary or important now. He moved out, leaving me with our three children. One was in college, another in high school, and the youngest in junior high. I explained to the children that we could either get bitter or be better, and I recommended we go for the "be better" because God said in *Hebrews 13:5, "Never will I leave you; never will I forsake you."*

I Only Have a Minute ... So Let's Make It Matter!

God kept His promise. Whenever I needed help, God showed up in the form of other people who became His hands and feet. I really believe you become more "usable" once you have gone through valleys yourself and know the depth of suffering that grief can bring. I sure felt weak when it came to thinking about raising the children alone and putting them through college! *II Corinthians 12:9* gave me strength: *"My grace is sufficient for you, for My strength is made perfect in weakness."* You become more willing to help those in need because you have a deeper understanding of what being in need feels like.

I don't pretend to know or understand all that God does in our lives or why He allows it, but I am grateful for how He cares for us through the trials. When God commissions, He empowers. Live His love in every area of your life and you will be amazed at the opportunities that just show up for you to serve others, which brings an inner joy that you know can only be from Him.

After a couple of years of immersing myself in work and the children's activities, I knew that it was time to be around other adults socially. A friend I worked with said her church had just started a new business singles group and wondered if I wanted to meet her there. That sounded like an ideal place to start meeting other people who were single and in my age group. My friend knew I was a speaker and asked, at that first meeting, if I would mind warming up the group. The men were on one side and the women were on the other side, just like in high school! I agreed, not knowing what would leap from my lips on such short notice. I turned to my now husband and said, "Sir, would you mind starting us out. Please tell us your name, age, weight, and how much money you make."

> **When God commissions, He empowers.**

Good Grief

Ken's eyes rolled back in disbelief, but quickly rallied replying, "My name is Ken, I'm younger than I look, I weigh more than I should, and I don't make what I'm worth." The group laughed and cheered. What a great answer and on such short notice! This man began to win my heart, which he captured completely when I became his wife in 1993.

Our wedding party was made up of our five children. My children all have weird but wonderful senses of humor which can show up quite unexpectedly. My oldest son, Jeff, walked me down the aisle at our wedding, and just before he turned me over to Ken at the altar, Jeff leaned forward and said to Ken, "There are no exchanges, no returns. She is an irregular." Ken and I began to laugh quietly as it really wasn't the place or time for one of those milk snorting, belly grabbing laughs which could easily have occurred.

> **Every loss brings pain and disruption into our lives.**

Ken and I have many wonderful memories together along with incredible grandchildren from all of our now-married children who have blessed us beyond belief! The experience of loving someone again deeply is a healthy way to get practice in giving and sharing your life with others. It also encourages us to hope. We can always hope everything will work out and we will have the people we love in our lives for a very long time. Our affection for one another grows out of the time we spend together. Time waters relationships, which are like flowers, causing them to grow and develop stronger roots. We are called to be rooted and grounded in our faith so, when loss comes, our faith will overcome our fears as we seek to understand our Savior with an even greater depth.

Every loss brings pain and disruption into our lives. Death is no stranger, but the closer the person is to you the greater the impact his or her death has on your life. Grief is a common thread that links us all together as we walk through the valley of shadows. We can't avoid it, but we can choose the way in which we approach it. We can fight it, struggle through it, or embrace it. If we understand what to expect as we grieve, we may find comfort and hope more readily than if we blindly let our emotions control our lives.

Grief is a normal process, but while we are grieving, our abilities are overshadowed, and the grief becomes the way we see life. It weighs us down and deadens our senses. We do learn from grief, which is a great teacher. Our lives are forever changed! Grief is like a wave that comes rolling in from a far-off place. It is an exercise in futility to fight it. The more you accept it, hold out your arms to it, and even embrace it, the quicker you will recover. Yield to your grief. Let it do its work in your life and mourn. It has been labeled everything from intense mental anguish to acute sorrow to deep remorse. It's a feeling of heaviness, or it was for me, anyway. I experienced an overwhelming weight on my chest that caused me to cry in gasps after the triplets died. The following poem by Edgar A. Guest is one that I have given to friends when they have lost a child. It was a comfort to me as well:

To All Parents

"I'll loan you for a little time
A child of Mine," He said,
"For you to love the while he lives
And mourn for when he's dead.

It may be six or seven years,
Or twenty two or three;
But will you, 'til I call him back,
Take care of him for Me?

Good Grief

He'll bring his charms to gladden you,
And should his stay be brief,
You'll have his loving memories
As solace for your grief.

I cannot promise he will stay,
Since all from earth return,
But there are lessons taught down there
I want this child to learn.

I've looked the wide world over
In my search for teachers true,
And, from all the throngs that crowd life's lanes,
I've selected you.

Now will you give him all your love,
Not think the labor vain,
Nor hate Me when I come to call
To take him back again?"

I fancied that I heard him say,
"Dear Lord, Thy will be done!"
For all the joy this child shall bring,
The risk of grief we'll run.

We'll shelter him with tenderness,
We'll love him while we may.
And for the happiness we've known,
Forever grateful stay.

But should the angels call for him
Sooner than we've planned,
We'll brave the bitter grief that comes,
And try to understand."

I Only Have a Minute ... So Let's Make It Matter!

The death of a friend is one that others, unfortunately, often do not recognize or support the same as when the loss has been a family member. Harold Ivan Smith expressed a wonderful sentiment to this end. "My friends, although dead, fill the bleachers of my memories. Experiencing my friend's death has depleted my heart. My heart lies collapsed, like a party balloon the morning after the celebration. No one understands my grief. I guess that is what I get for taking friendship so seriously." We choose our friends and quite often become closer to them than we are to many of our relatives.

At one of the "landmark" birthday parties for my best friend from high school, Jan, I dressed up as a bag lady and crashed the party. My flowered dress with yellow short ankle nylons tucked into sturdy black shoes made for an interesting fashion statement. A black straw hat

> **Show and tell your family and friends at every opportunity that you love them.**

with a ribbon along with granny glasses and a classy beaded bag completed the ensemble. I gave a little monologue about being old, and then, in closing, recited the following poem:

> *Of all the friends I've ever met,*
> *You are the one I won't forget.*
> *And If I die before you do,*
> *I'll go to heaven and wait for you.*

We then hugged enthusiastically, knowing that we really do care a LOT about each other! We have both chosen to make the investment of our time, energy, and commitment to caring, sharing, and loving one another as we journey through this uncertain world. Besides, we have to be forever friends because we both know too much about each other. Show and tell your family and friends at every opportunity that you love them. The more unique the way is that you tell them, the longer they will remember what you said.

Once I was actually paid to be a bag lady at a park pavilion for a lady who was turning 50 years old. Her family wanted her to really remember this birthday. I did my best. I remember strolling around the benches and tables saying how good the food looked. The mother of the birthday girl, not knowing I was hired to do this, told her daughter to put together a plate of food for me. I then burst into a song and the monologue, much to the shock, delight and relief of the "birthday girl." What made this an even more memorable event to me was that, just as I was leaving, there was a legitimate "bag man" standing by a garbage can I had to pass by on the way back to my car. As I walked by, still in character, he winked at me. I grinned and strolled into the parking lot feeling pretty good that someone out there thought I was a "hottie." A compliment is a compliment. I digress. How unlike me ... let's get back to finding the good in grief.

> The only thing that no one can ever take away from you is what you have become!

The Scriptures teach that God will use suffering to build character and to purify our faith (see *Romans 5* and *I Peter 1*). Change. Growth. Healing. Beauty for ashes. Gladness for mourning. Praise out of despair. But the last phrase is all-important: that it might be to His glory, "for the display of his splendor." The only thing that no one can ever take away from you is what you have become! You are a product of your choices. God didn't promise days without pain, laughter without sorrow, sun without rain, but He did promise strength for the day, comfort for the tears, and light for the way. "If God brings you to it, He will bring you through it." Barbara Ascher said it well: "*I have been trying to make the best of grief and am just beginning to learn to allow it to make the best of me."*

A companion of grief is pain, which is often fought with denial, which is much more than a river in Egypt. Denial is used to block out the unthinkable, but it brings with it the fear of the unknown since you are denying the reality of what happened. Denial is a cushion which may help for a short time but it keeps you from moving on. It

> Positive memories are the gifts we leave our loved ones.

helps to deal with your pain a little bit at a time. Everyone grieves and heals differently. Some want to be connected to people while others prefer to be left alone. It will take effort, but letting other people know what you need, as well as how they can help you, is both healthy and healing.

One way that dear friends of ours coped with the loss of a premature infant was to use a small box, which one of the grandfathers had lovingly made. They placed memorabilia of the dear little one's life inside along with a note to their baby. This can be very healing as it gives the baby its own identity as a family member who will never be forgotten. On the anniversary of the death of their child, they bring out the box and talk about their feelings. It is both a time to reflect and a time to heal.

There are now funeral homes with personalized memorial services which surround the dearly departed with some of their personal effects that tell about their lives. One lady had her sewing machine near the casket with a couple pieces of the lovely handiwork she crafted. Some places have large TV screens available that can show personalized family-produced video. That is a wonderful way for those who didn't know the deceased very well to join in the celebration of her life. That funeral home will take up to 50 family photos and put them into a DVD where they fade into one another with music. Music provides vibrational healing, which helps relax the family members and friends as they grieve. This takes the place of the old picture board. Ways to express our love and grief can be woven together into a memorable celebration of our loved one's life. The more unique, the longer remembered.

Doris "Cousin Tuny" Freeman is an 81 year old lady who, after her beloved husband, W.C. Harris, passed, made a peace garden in her backyard which is filled with concrete angels, squirrels, chipmunks, toads, birdbaths, and of course, Jesus. Everything in the garden has a story which holds a special memory. It could also be called yard art. The garden is an oasis of peace and happiness. She loves to go and just "sit a spell" while she reflects on all the fun, upbeat memories, which are brought back as she gazes about her beautiful garden. The garden is a sanctuary of love and peaceful reflection. Our loved ones live on in our memories. We sense their presence in the silent place within our soul that still whispers their names.

Positive memories are the gifts we leave our loved ones. Try to create some everyday because even a healthy lifestyle does not guarantee a long life. Reconcile conflicts and replace them with forgiveness and joy. Feed your soul with friends. To be a better friend don't look backward or forward ... look inward and what do you see? Socrates said, "Above all else, know thyself." Knowing yourself will help you sort out the best way for you to grieve the inevitable losses of life yet to come.

Did you know that after death your body is like a peanut shell? The shell is left ... and the nut is gone. That may very well be on my tombstone. It would be one way to "leave them laughing." One of my loved ones may even comment ... **"Good Grief!"**

May you grow from your grief so that you, in turn, can lift someone else from their grief to higher ground through God's abundant love, now dwelling even deeper within you.

Chapter Seven
Don't Wait – Celebrate!

We need to start having the time of our lives right now because this is the only moment we can count on. Why put off enjoying yourself when there is fun a-foot and all that is missing is you? Don't miss out on having the biggest smile and the last laugh for the day.

We need to celebrate this gift we call life which should be lived as a celebration. Did you know that your work should be a celebration of who you are?

Take time to count all of your blessings each day. In fact, write them in one of those beautiful blank books and call it your "Blessing Book." Whenever you start feeling sorry for yourself for whatever reason, go and read your Blessing Book. You will hopefully soon be able to say, "I am TOO blessed to be stressed" and mean it! I have also heard of people keeping all the thank you cards they receive to read gain on days when they don't feel appreciated, are bored, or feel unimportant in the big scheme of things.

Life is only dull and boring to dull and boring people. Shut off the television and be interesting yourself. Reading is a wonderful way to take a trip in your mind where you can chose the destination by the book you pick. Physical traveling is a great education as well. One of the best parts of every vacation my husband

I Only Have a Minute ... So Let's Make It Matter!

and I take are the wonderful people we meet along the way. Ask people what they are all about and get ready to hear unique stories crafted from the life they have lived up until that very moment with you.

People have fun in a variety of ways. Research shows that if you get and stay friendly, you will live longer and enjoy it a lot more! Getting out in the sun raises your serotonin which gives your mood a boost. I no longer like to just sit in the sun as I did when I was a teenager craving the perfect tan, but I do like to be outside because it is more stimulating. There seems to be a lot more activity to invigorate our senses when we are outside. I know I'm getting older, not only because people cheerfully remind me whenever they get the chance, but also because I am starting to watch birds. I call my husband from any room in the house to hurry up and come see the beautiful bird with the red head out at the bird feeder. The kids bought us a bird book for Christmas. I think that seals it. Thank God we have our will made out!

> Laughter is life's lubricant and the music of our souls.

Laughter is life's lubricant and the music of our souls. Music provides a soothing as well as healing effect for a variety of ailments or mood blips. I know for a fact that calming music, especially gospel music, has been proven to enhance the healing process in the intensive care units at several hospitals. I personally think the antibodies get saved, become evangelists, and work harder to heal the person!

We don't stop laughing because we get old. We get old because we stop laughing. Soap is to the body what laughter is to the mind. Do you know what happens if you don't laugh? That unexpressed energy turns to cellulite and falls to your hips. I can't afford that, so I laugh a lot and my cellulite applauds by hitting against itself when I do sit-ups.

It has been said that humor is a regression to our childhood. Growing old is inevitable, but growing up is optional. I do believe that we are overworked and underplayed. Remember that "He who dies with the most toys is still dead." The point in that statement is that you are not going to stay alive any longer because you have cool stuff, but you may stay around a little longer if you just play more.

Play is nature's way of training us for what life has in store. Play serves more than thirty developmental functions – from motor skills like running, jumping and balancing to cognitive skills like creativity, logic and problem-solving to self-esteem, according to Prof. Gordon Burghardt from the University of Tennessee. Play is a fundamental need, just like air, water, and the five food groups. Yet our current lifestyle makes play a luxury few of us can afford, time-wise. We need to inject playful moments into the things we are already doing. Laughter and togetherness are key to our health, growth, and relationships, which are all well worth celebrating! Thinking playfully is the ignition that starts things off even if it is only for a short recess during the day.

> **Play is nature's way of training us for what life has in store.**

I was driving along and drove by a funeral home. That isn't particularly funny but the name of the funeral home was "Amigone." I stood there and commented, "Yes, you are or you wouldn't be there!" We medical people are known for our sick humor. A bandage over our mouth is a last resort but sometimes a necessary one. It does, however, beat an ace wrap with those little clips.

I Only Have a Minute ... So Let's Make It Matter!

Don't wait to do fun things with the people you care about and whose company you enjoy! Each age or stage of life offers something unique that needs to be grasped immediately and enjoyed fully while we are still here to enjoy both the person and the experience. I ran across a poem that makes this point well. It is appropriately titled "The Time is Now," which seems to fit in perfectly right now:

> If you are ever going to love me,
> Love me now, while I can know
> The sweet and tender feelings
> Which from true affection flow.
>
> Love me now
> While I'm living.
> Do not wait until I'm gone
> And then have it chiseled in marble,
> Sweet words on ice-cold stone.
>
> If you have tender thoughts of me,
> Please tell me now.
> If you wait until I am sleeping,
> Never to awaken,
> There will be death between us,
> And I won't hear you then.
>
> So, if you love me, even a little bit,
> Let me know it while I am living
> So I can treasure it.
>
> *- Anon.*

* * *

Naomi Judd said, "Sixty is the new forty ... or less!" We are aging better these days with all the breakthroughs in modern medicine along with the increased knowledge available to us by way of the Internet, which has improved worldwide communication. That can be good and bad as we are almost instantly aware of what's going on around the world. Let's just say that the Girl Scout awards don't make national news. "If it bleeds, it leads" is all too common in the media.

People enrich their lives when they celebrate together when things go right. We also help to divide the inevitable burdens when things go wrong or become unbearable. Nutritious friends help you to grow. They help you laugh with life. Negative people try to steal your joy. That reminds me of this really negative guy who got on an airplane. He arrived late and boarded the plane complaining that he had an aisle seat. As the flight progressed, lunch arrived. (This is a very old story, as you can now tell, because these were the days when they served meals in coach, more popularly known as the "cheap seats.")

Anyway, the lunch turned out to be a turkey sandwich. He looked at the sandwich and immediately put on the light to summon the stewardess. "I can't eat this sandwich," he complained. "This is a bad sandwich. What are you going to do about it?" She picked up the sandwich and started to spank it saying, "Bad sandwich, bad sandwich." He looked her in the eye and asked what his options were. She replied, "You can go in back and make something yourself, have nothing, or go 'out' for something." The people sitting around Mr. Happy started to laugh.

> **Nutritious friends help you to grow. They help you laugh with life.**

A gentleman went up to the stewardess later complimenting her on how she handled the man. She said she has been saying similar things for years, i.e., last week it was bad chicken, bad chicken, etc. She then commented that you just have to go-with-the-flow. You have to stay flexible so you don't get bent out of shape. Remember when someone pushes your buttons that YOU are the one who installed them! You choose what bothers you. How true that is! We can't afford to let negative people steal our moments of joy. Life is too short!

For that very reason we all need to be busy building memories! It feels good to make others happy ... and then join with them in the merriment! We will then forget about our own concerns. We should not dwell on what other generations are doing to make us crazy, either. To some teenagers, getting out of bed is a career move.

> **Life is not about what you leave TO your children and grandchildren. It is about what you leave 'IN them' that really matters.**

Journal funny things that happen in your family. We think we won't forget because it was the funniest thing we have ever seen, but time passes and the mind takes short vacations every now and then. That reminds me of the story about a young boy who was on his way upstairs. He stopped, turned around and said to the rest of his family, "I'm going up to pray. Does anyone want anything?" That may be a gentle reminder to us that our prayers should not just be laundry lists of what we want, but more like thank you cards for all that we all ready have.

Life is not about what you leave to your children and grandchildren. It is about what you leave "in them" that really matters! Think of yourself as a treasured gift to your family, a history book filled with wisdom and bound with love. There is no time like the present – and no present like your time!

Craft a life that matters in the moments and the minutes you live. Don't count on next week, next month, or next year.

Don't Wait - Celebrate!

Your math, as well as your path in life, may be suddenly changed without prior notice. Life is like food with an undetermined expiration date. Don't let the fruit of your life get spoiled by self indulgence. Fill yourself with the preservatives found in Scripture that will help you enjoy a life filled with love, joy, peace, and contentment. Let the abundance of your life spill, like a water fall into the lives of those around you to bring joy, peace and hope ... even if you Only Have A Minute. Take The Time ... And Make It Matter!

In Closing...

Moments can matter more than we think at the time they are happening. Our job is to stay tuned in to what is going on around us so we don't miss a miracle in process. We commit the sin of omission when we don't take the time to make a difference in the lives of others.

We also need to fully appreciate the significance of a moment and what it can mean if we care enough to take the time to make the most of it. You may be thinking…how DO I make the most of a moment? My advice: Be fully "in it." Be engaged with what you are doing, thinking, and feeling so much that you are filled up for the moment until you release the love within yourself so that it can flow freely into the lives of others. I just did that as I wrote this book.

Now it is your turn to release the lessons that you have learned into practical life applications for the benefit of others. Look for ways to show kindness every day in many ways. Don't miss an opportunity to become contagious in ways that bring cheer and give hope to the sad and disheartened while, at the same time, being sensitive to their possible unspoken needs for love and inner peace. Just being with someone in their "moment of need" may give them peace with your presence. It may be just enough because you Took The Time … And It Mattered …

even if it was for Only A Minute!

Biography

Kathy Brown, RN, CSP, is an international keynote speaker, author, and seminar leader. Her background as a communications coordinator, development and training specialist, registered nurse, corporate recruiter, and business owner brings a wealth of information along with real life experiences that have inspired and motivated hundreds of audiences nationwide.

Kathy has earned the prestigious Certified Speaking Professional designation which is the speaking industry's international measure of professional platform skill. Only about 8 percent of all professional speakers hold this professional designation.

Her first book, *"Living Happily Ever Laughter – A Guide To Thinking Funny In A Fast Paced World,"* is a very fun, motivational cartoon gift book in its third printing.

Kathy has humorously inspired and motivated clients such as 3M, Miami Children's Hospital, Sprint, Thomson Delmar Learning, Baptist Hospital - Pensacola, Cornell University, Care Providers, IBM Mid America, Bethel College, Norwest Bank, Medtronic, Wesley Health Care Ministries, Blue Cross & Blue Shield, Northwest Airlines, and Medica, to name a few.

Energetically Speaking
888.524.5194
651.730.1109
www.kathybrown.com